The Perfect Pipe

The Perfect Pipe

H. PAUL JEFFERS

with drawings and photography by
KEVIN GORDON

BURFORD BOOKS

For Hy Turner

Printed in the United States of America

10 9 8 7 6 5 4 3 2 1

Library of Congress Cataloging-in-Publication Data

Jeffers, H. Paul (Harry Paul), 1934–
    The perfect pipe / H. Paul Jeffers: with drawings and photography by
Kevin Gordon.
        p. cm.
    Includes bibliographical references and index.
    ISBN 1-58080-065-3 (hardcover)
    1. Tobacco pipes. 2. Smoking. I. Title.
TS2270.J44   1998
688'.42—dc21   98-27065
                                                     CIP

Through the haze I had a vague vision of Holmes in his dressing gown coiled up in an armchair with his black clay pipe between his lips.

—DR. JOHN H. WATSON
The Hound of the Baskervilles

The Perfect Pipe

Contents

Introduction   Pipe Bowl 1

One   Virginia's Kingly Plant 9

Two   O Blessed Pipe 23

Three   The Gentlemanly Smoke 49

Four   Anatomy of the Pipe 61

Five   A Sweet Smoke 87

Six   Put This in Your Pipe 117

Seven   Pouches, Jars, Racks, Reamers,

                 Tampers, and Other Gadgetry 127

Eight   When and Where 135

Nine   The Delight of the Pipe 145

Ten   Pipe Dreams 173

The Last Pipe 194

Glossary 195

Further Reading 199

Sources 201

Index 207

Introduction

Pipe Bowl

Old pipe of mine, for many a year
    What boon companions we have been!
With here a smile and there a tear,
    How many changes we have seen!
How many hearts have ceased to beat,
    How many eyes have ceased to shine,
How many friends will never meet,
    Since first we met, old pipe of mine!

—JOHN J. GORMLEY
Old Pipe of Mine

*A*top a table beside the chair where I read (not enough) and watch TV (far too much) squats a large wooden salad bowl, which several years ago found itself converted to a convenient within-arm's-reach receptacle for my pipes. It holds about a dozen that are fairly new and a few very sturdy ones that date back over forty years. Whether fresh or many-seasoned, each evokes memories of the events, places, and people of my four decades of puffing.

The latest, a Peterson's sandblasted briar with a straight stem and sterling-silver band, was a gift from my literary agent, Jake Elwell. The oldest came from L. J. Peretti's tobacco store in Boston and was presented by students in a journalism class that I taught at Boston University. There is a Dunhill given to me by editors, writers, and announcers of the all-news radio station WINS on the occasion of my leaving for another broadcasting job in 1974. The bowl also holds an elegant Prince. Being part Welsh in ancestry, I bought it on the day that Charles, Prince of Wales, married Lady Diana Spencer. The pipe is now retired, having been smoked for the last time while, along with the rest of the world, I watched the telecast from Westminster Abbey of the funeral of Diana, Princess of Wales.

At the University of Iowa in the 1950s there were smoke-filled late-night hours working on my master's thesis. Wearing an army uniform, I smoked pipes in bars on Cannery Row in Monterey, California, while listening to stories about pipe-smoking author John Steinbeck and wondering if I would ever see my name on a book jacket. Then came pipes in my faculty office at B.U. and in the WHDH-TV newsroom in the town of the Kennedys and the Boston Strangler in the early 1960s. In the ABC Radio newsroom stories involved Vietnam and the Civil Rights movement. Working at NBC in the late 1970s and CBS in the Reagan years, chasing the news across the country and around the world, I never left home without a couple of pipes and a supply of tobacco in my pockets or suitcases. When I returned, I usually had at least one pipe that I'd bought to remind me as I lit it of where I'd been and why, of what I'd done, and of the interesting people I'd met.

Pipes in the bowl have been clenched in my teeth while I worked at becoming a writer of books, first on a Smith-Corona portable typewriter, then on a full-size Royal electric, and ultimately on a computer. Success and progress in a day's writing were measured by how much I smoked. If the work was not proceeding well I stopped often to puff and think while struggling to press on. A good day was the one in which, after a few hours, the pipe was still in my mouth with the tobacco having been consumed and the pipe bowl gone cold without my having noticed.

Not in my chairside bowl but resting in a special holder is a huge yellow calabash given to me by a broadcasting colleague to mark the occasion of the publication of my first mystery novel. The yarn brought together two of my favorite characters. One's life read like fiction—Teddy Roosevelt. The other was imaginary but seemed real—Sherlock Holmes. Displayed next to the big calabash are two pipes with Holmes's image carved in meerschaum. Neither has been smoked. One was bought in a pipe shop in Baker Street, London, strictly as an addition to my collection of Sherlockiana. The second, a Christmas gift from my sister Arlene, hangs on a wall and is encased in a protective box, not so much as a sign of my regard for Holmes as my affection for her.

Unfortunately, pipes have not always been associated with happy memories. Looking at the calabash, I am reminded that a few years after the friend gave it to me, he chose to end his life without explaining why. Arlene's Sherlockian meerschaum evokes a memory of her husband with his favorite pipe resting in his hand as he was buried long before anyone expected him to be. One of the young men at WINS who had contributed to my going-away pipe died a few years later of AIDS.

But most of the pipes are as caked with happy memories as they are with burned tobacco. They include my fledgling stabs at the art of pipe smoking when I was an undergraduate at Temple University. The pipe was a cheap one bought in a drugstore, along with a paper pouch of inexpensive tobacco. The attempt was made in secret, and wisely so, because I had not a clue as to what I was doing. Subsequently I got the knack, and I have been puffing away ever since with much better pipes and decidedly more upscale tobacco.

In my decades of pipe smoking I have passed incalculable hours in the pleasant company of like-minded friends, such as Hy Turner. A veteran journalist and historian of the newspapers of New York City, he regaled me with stories of the rough-and-tumble days of reporters who never went out to get a story without making sure their pockets contained a pipe or two. My journalistic idols, it seemed, were all pipe smokers, from Richard Harding Davis trekking along with Teddy Roosevelt's Rough Riders in Cuba during the Spanish-American War to Walter Cronkite on TV reporting the latest space shot from Cape Canaveral. For a young man such as I, working to make a career in news, a pipe seemed as great a necessity as a notebook and pencil. And as a would-be author I had literary idols, too, who smoked pipes—Mark Twain, John Steinbeck, Robert Benchley, and the one I admired most during my undergraduate years, Pennsylvania's own John O'Hara.

Others who imbued me with the love of pipes were found not among authors or in my circle of personal friends and colleagues in news, but on the screens of the Colonial and Rialto Theaters when I was growing up in Phoenixville, Pennsylvania, from Clark Gable and Errol Flynn to Fred MacMurray and Bing Crosby. And of course, Sherlock Holmes was up there on the screen in the person of Basil Rathbone, smoking not a cumbersome calabash but what I was to recognize later as a Peterson briar made in Dublin.

Reminding me of my Irish-Welsh ancestry, and informing me that pipe smoking was a Celtic tradition, were Barry Fitzgerald in *The Quiet Man* and Walter Pidgeon as the Welsh pastor and Donald Crisp as the patriarch of the coal-mining Morgan family in *How Green Was My Valley*.

High school memories include "Pop" Rhodes, who puffed a big black pipe with extreme patience while I struggled to grasp the mysteries of his courses in chemistry and physics. Many college professors affected the image of the pipe smoker as intellectual.

Inevitably, my pipe and I encountered the zealotry of the anti-smoking people. While I was standing in line at the check-out counter of a drugstore in Syracuse in 1974 a young woman ahead of me looked with horror at the pipe in my mouth. "Oh God! Smoke," she gasped, dropping her items. As she ran off without making a purchase, I had no chance to show her that not only was my pipe not lit, but its bowl was empty. A few years later at a journalism convention, the wife of my boss gazed at my pipe, made a sour face, and asserted, "I do not permit smoking anywhere near me." Being a gentleman, I put away my unlit pipe, but not without wondering what domestic life must have been like for her husband, who smoked at work like the proverbial chimney.

While these people and others like them are entitled to their views on smoking, and while I respect their opinions, I am convinced that their adamant refusal to accept my right to enjoy a pipe (or cigar) is symptomatic of a deep unhappiness that finds expression in their

This 1887 painting by John Wallace, which shows a man relaxing with a pipe and a book, became the frontis-piece for Pipe and Pouch, The Smoker's Own Book of Poetry, *compiled by John Knight in 1895.*

inability to accept the idea that somewhere, somone might be enjoying himself. When confronted by such people, I recall an old poem, "The Ballad of the Pipe," by Hermann Rave:

> Let others fret and fume with care.
> 'Tis easy finding everywhere,
>   But happiness is rarer;
> And if I find it sweet and ripe,
> In this tobacco and my pipe,
>   I'll count it all the fairer.

Throughout this book you will read many happy things about pipes, how and why the pipe came into existence, and the reasons why pipe smoking has remained a part of the human experience, and an especially American phenomenon, for centuries. Beginning with the history of tobacco in general and pipe smoking in particular, it deals with all aspects of the world of pipes—kinds and types, how they are made, choosing them, and how to fully enjoy them.

As the nineteenth-century English writer Lord Bulwer-Lytton pointed out in *Night and Morning,* "A pipe is a great soother, a pleasant comforter." For proof, consider an evening in 1833 when Carlyle and Emerson sat in silence for many hours in front of a fireplace, puffing soberly till midnight, and then parted, shaking hands in mutual congratulation on sharing their profitable and pleasant evening.

As you read this book, do so in the spirit of the poet Richard le Gallienne, who penned:

> And though one's eyes will dream astray,
> And lips forget to sue or sway,
> It is enough to merely be,
>   With Pipe and Book.

In that spirit this book celebrates both pipes and those who choose to smoke them, whether they are old hands with a pipe or novices, and illuminates what it is about pipe smoking that has been so attractive to so many people for so long.

1

Virginia's Kingly Plant

Oh, muse! grant me the power
I have the will to sing
How oft in lonely hour,
When storms would round me lower,
Tobacco's proved a king!

—ANONYMOUS

When I was a boy there was a prank I and my friends pulled in which one of us phoned a tobacco store and inquired, "Do you have Sir Walter Raleigh in a can?" If the answer was yes, the caller, to the accompaniment of his conspirators' guffaws and giggles, demanded, "Well, let him out!"

The only portrait of Sir Walter Raleigh published during his lifetime, from The History of the World, *1617. The object in his hand does not appear to be a pipe.*
New York Public Library

That Raleigh's name might someday achieve immortality as a brand of pipe tobacco hardly could have occurred to Sir Walter when, according to tradition, he introduced the English-speaking world to pipe smoking. Having tasted tobacco and found it to his liking, he immediately recognized the plant's potential as a moneymaker for a patch of land in the New World that had been claimed for England by explorers and named for Queen Elizabeth I, the "Virgin Queen."

But even before Raleigh's adventurers arrived in Virginia, other English explorers had made note of a peculiar practice of the American natives. Sir John Hawkins wrote in 1564 the inhabitants "have a kinde of herbe dryed, which with a cane, and an earthen cup in the end, and the dried herbs put together do smoke thro the cane the smoke thereof." Hawkins tried it and carried samples of both the herb and the smoking implement home. However, there is nothing to indicate that pipe smoking caught fire in England. Eight years later William Harrison, another Englishman on a trek into the American wilds, observed "the taking in of smoke of the Indian herbe called Tobacco, by an instrument formed like a little ladel, whereby it passeth from the mouth into the head and stomach."

The first written account of Englishmen smoking on British soil speaks of Captain William Middleton and two other seafarers, a Captain Thomas Price and a Captain Koet, who "drank tobacco publickly in London and that Londoners flocked from all parts to see them." No date was given for this bold act, and no particulars were noted.

It was not until a 1584 expedition to America under command of Sir Richard Grenville and Ralph Lane that the possibility of making money from tobacco growing was investigated. One Thomas Hariot, along for the ride, wrote a report on agriculture that might be exploited.

In "A briefe and true report on the new found land of Virginia" he noted "an herbe which is sowed that in the West Indies hath divers names according to the severall places and countries where it groweth and is used. The Spaniardes generally call it Tobacco. The leaves thereof being dried and brought into powder, they take the fume or smoke there–of by sucking it thro pipes made of claie into their stomacke and heade."

While Hariot extolled the medicinal virtues of tobacco, he also pointed out the pleasurable aspects of pipe smoking. "We ourselves during the time we were there," he wrote, "used to suck it after their manner, as also since our returne, and have found manie rare and wonderful experiments of the vertues thereof."

THE WAGER DECIDED

A nineteenth-century drawing illustrates the historic wager between Queen Elizabeth I and Sir Walter Raleigh, who bet the Queen that he could weigh smoke. The Queen paid up.
New York Public Library

Hariot's companion on the voyage, Ralph Lane, did more than write about tobacco: He showed Raleigh how to smoke it. Wasting no time in becoming an evangelist for tobacco, Sir Walter cajoled the monarch into taking a few puffs. Then he bet the queen that he could weigh the smoke of his pipe. When the bemused monarch took him up on the wager, he began by weighing his fully packed pipe. He then smoked it until only a little ash remained in the bowl and placed the pipe on the scale again. The difference in the weights, he claimed, was the weight of the smoke.

As the Virgin Queen paid the piper she quipped, "Many al-

chemists have turned gold into smoke, but Raleigh is the first who
has turned smoke into gold."

Encouraged by the results of the 1584 venture, Raleigh sent a second expedition to Virginia the following spring. This time Grenville
left Lane and a handful of men behind, but the settlement ran into
troubles with Indians. The men had to be rescued. When Grenville
tried again, leaving fifteen souls to establish a settlement at Roanoke,
the settlers vanished without a trace. The episode is recorded in history as the "The Lost Colony."

It was not until 1607 that England succeeded in establishing a per-
manent colony at Jamestown. The leader of this hardy group, Captain
John Smith, urged the colonists to grow maize (corn). But another
leader of the struggling settlement, John Rolfe, thought he saw greater
chance for success in the cultivation of the plant that had been lauded
by Lane and Hariot and promoted by Raleigh.

The Colonist and the Princess

While securing a place for himself in the history of tobacco as
Virginia's first colonial planter, Rolfe is best known as the man who
married the beautiful seventeen-year-old daughter of the Indian king
Powhatan. She was called Matowaka, but her nickname was Pocahontas, which translated to something like "Frisky." At the time the
princess met Rolfe she was the wife of a warrior named Kocoum. To
safeguard the colony against the Indians, the governor of Virginia, Sir
Thomas Dale, had Pocahontas kidnapped and held as a hostage. She
proved successful not only in staving off an attack by her father's warriors and being rescued by her considerably older husband, but also
in teaching her captors how to remain alive by living off the land.

"Blessed Pocahontas," wrote John Smith. "She, under God, was the instrument to preserve this colony from death, famine, and utter confusion."

As a means of maintaining peace with the Indians, Rolfe took Pocahontas as his wife. They settled at Varina, near present-day Richmond, and enjoyed a happy marriage. Whether she smoked a pipe is open to conjecture. But there is no doubting that when Rolfe took her to England she became the darling of Elizabeth I and her courtiers, including Raleigh. However, it was what Rolfe had to say about the possibilities of tobacco as a cash crop that really got Sir Walter fired up.

English legend holds that as he put a flame to the tobacco in a pipe bowl for the first time he said to his servant, "Mr. Ridley, we are today lighting a candle in England which by God's blessing will never be put out."

Four years after he took his first puff from a pipe, equally prescient craftsmen were setting up shops to make clay pipes to handle the influx of tobacco from Virginia.

As to Raleigh's smoking habits, the magazine *British Apollo* reported in 1708 that he "indulged himself in Smoking two pipes a Day." Published ninety years after Raleigh's death, the article left posterity an amusing yarn that may or may not be true. The author claimed that when a "simple fellow" saw smoke pouring from Raleigh's mouth, he thought Sir Walter was on fire and promptly doused him with the contents of a tankard of ale. A later version of the story had Raleigh being drenched with a large bucket of water.

The soaked figure in this tale has also been identified as the Elizabethan comedian Richard Tarlton in 1611. And the story was included in Barnaby Rich's "Irish Hubub," printed in 1619, in which the douser was a "certain Welshman coming newly to London" and encountering a pipe smoker for the first time. The extinguishing liquid was a "bowl of beere."

Raleigh's first public pipe smoking has been placed in various locations: on a dock in Penzance, the Virginia Inn on the Somerset-Dorset border, and the Pied Bull at Islington near London.

Another story has Raleigh smoking a pipe in the company of Shakespeare and Bacon at a house in Durham, England. The "new Indian weed" was quaffed from silver bowls as the trio discussed "the highest themes in poetry and science, while gazing upon the flower beds and the river, the darting barges of dame and cavalier, and the

It was said, but never proved, that when a servant found Sir Walter Raleigh smoking, he thought Sir Walter was on fire—so he immediately doused him with beer.
University of North Carolina Collection

Sketches purported to be Raleigh smoking clay pipes.
New York Public Library

distant pavilions of the Globe," the London theater in which Shakespeare's plays were produced.

In lore, legend, and fact, the location where Raleigh first smoked his pipe in public has been claimed by at least as many inns and private homes as American addresses that hung out signs boasting, GEORGE WASHINGTON SLEPT HERE.

Raleigh's only written mention of tobacco was in 1618. On the return of one of his ships from Virginia he referred to the tobacco remaining aboard in bundles called roles. He wrote, "Sir Lewis Stukely sold all the tobacco at Plimouth of which, for the most part of it, I gave him a fift part of it, as also a role for my Lord Admirall and a role for himself."

The last time Raleigh smoked in public was that same year. It was immediately before he was beheaded on the orders of the successor to Elizabeth I's throne, King James I, who hated both Raleigh and what James called the "stinking weed" that Sir Walter had so vigorously and joyfully promoted.

So successful had he been in popularizing tobacco that as Raleigh went to the headsman's chopping block, pipe smoking was accepted by all the social classes throughout King James's realm.

A 1640 poem, "Wits' Recreations," went:

Tobacco engages
Both sexes, all ages,
  The poor as well as the wealthy;
From the court to the cottage,
From childhood to dotage,
  Both those that are sick and the healthy.

Good as Gold

Even before Pocahontas took England by storm and her husband excited Raleigh as to the profits to be made by cultivating tobacco in Virginia, smoking had become so popular through Europe that in 1602 someone wrote, "This precious herbe, TABACCO most divine, the sweete and sole delight of mortall men. . . ."

Especially *business* men. Some of these lost no time in organizing a joint-stock venture (the Virginia Company) to foster trade in tobacco. As a result, Captain John Smith soon complained to the company that corn planting was being abandoned in favor of tobacco, which sold at six times what the planters got for corn.

When tobacco became the Virginia colony's only export, Governor Dale had to force the colonists to plant grain, reminding them that they could not eat money. Dissuading the growing of tobacco was a diffcult task that proved impossible when the profits kept pouring into the colony. While this influx made Rolfe a very wealthy man, his happiness was dimmed by the death of Pocahontas in England in 1617. Broken-hearted, Rolfe went back to the colony in which Virginia tobacco had become as good as gold—literally.

By 1619 production had reached twenty thousand pounds. Eight years later it amounted to half a million. In 1639 exports totaled a million and a half pounds. So important was tobacco that it supplanted gold as legal tender. It was accepted as payment for all commodities, taxes, fines, and other dues of the colony. If a man did not go to church, he was fined two hundred pounds of tobacco. Bondservants bought their freedom with it. The pay of carpenters was thirty pounds a day, but so many saw better opportunities in tobacco that they set aside saws and hammers to raise it, causing a shortage of builders.

There was also such an acute absence of wives for the men of Jamestown that when a shipload of English girls, described at the time as "ninety agreeable persons, young and incorrupt," arrived in 1619, eager bachelors paid 120 pounds of tobacco apiece as a marriage fee for a bride. The next year a cargo of "sixty maids of virtuous education, young and handsome," fetched 150 pounds of tobacco each.

"TABACCO Most Divine"

The scientific name for the tobacco found in Virginia is *Nicotiana*. It probably originated in Mexico. By the time of the advent of white men on North American soil, the plant was growing in all of the eastern half of the continent, immediately west of the Mississippi River, and in lower Canada. Its relatives in the world of plants are the petunia, potato, garden pepper, eggplant, and tomato. A tablespoonful of its tiny seeds can yield six and a half acres of tobacco.

Nicotiana inferta infundibulo ex quo hauriunt fumu Indi & nau cleri.

The tobacco plant, sketched in 1570.
New York Public Library

Its first use by the natives of the Americas had been in religious rituals. In Mexico tobacco was believed to be the incarnation of the wife of the god of rain and agriculture. Caribs in Brazil used it to instill courage in warriors. The Indians of Virginia hoped its smoke would appease the anger of gods and ensure abundant catches of fish. But with the plant so readily available at every turn to the general population, tobacco smoking did not remain the province of holy men very long.

The white intruders of the fifteenth century found it being smoked in three forms: Columbus's sailors and their successors saw the Taino inhabitants of Cuba and other islands smoking it as cigars; in Central and South America were tubes very much like latter-day cigarettes; and Mexican and North American Indians preferred pipes, many of them shaped into representations of human or other figures. The form of smoking that was carried back to Europe, therefore, was dictated by the type of smoking encountered. Because Spanish and Portuguese conquerers found the natives smoking rolled tobacco leaves, it was the cigar that

Pottery pipe from province of Esmeraldas, Ecuador.
New York Public Library

became the principal way of smoking in Spain and Portugal. Englishmen who settled the eastern coast of North America emulated the natives by taking up the pipe. Sailors of these seafaring, empire-building nations soon carried tobacco seeds to the four corners of the world, assuring that no matter where they landed around the globe there would be ample supplies of tobacco.

Initially—and to the dismay of the English—the world was more interested in the tobacco grown in the Spanish islands than in the Virginia variety, which was judged to be of such poor quality that even John Rolfe had to admit that the colony's "great store of tobacco (was) not of the highest kind . . . indeed, very poor." He wrote, "It grows not fully a yard above ground, bearing a little yellow flower, like to henbane . . . where-as the best tobacco of Trinidad is large, sharp, and growing two or three yards from the ground, bearing a flower of the breadth of our bell-flowers in England."

Consequently, in one of history's first cases of commercial piracy (no one knows how it was achieved; probably by bribery), Rolfe got his hands on some of the precious Spanish seeds, so that by 1612 Virginia was growing tobacco that even the most particular pipe smoker had to concede was pleasant, sweet, and strong. With good

Tobacco quickly became a hot commodity in taverns, inns, and alehouses. Dutch engraving, c. 1630.
New York Public Library

Virginia tobacco available, merchants sprang up everywhere to peddle it.

A 1613 writer noted that tobacco had become "a commodity that is now as vendible in every tavern, inn, and alehouse, as either wine, ale or beer, and for apothecaries, shops, grocers shops, chandlers shops (and others) that have no other trade to live by, but by selling tobacco."

Francis Bacon, King James's lord chancellor and a foe of tobacco smoking and that spiritous drink known as whiskey, spoke of the "intolerable number of ale houses [and] tobacco houses, and those that sell hot waters [whiskey], the one of them brought from the wild Irish [the Irish had invented whiskey distilling], and the other from the wild Indies [American tobacco]."

While Bacon and the tobaccophobic James hated the stuff and tried to quench its use through strict laws and heavy taxation, they were fighting a losing game. In *The Mighty Leaf* (1952) Jerome E. Brooks wrote, "In Virginia tobacco had become king." Indeed so. It dominated colonial life to a greater degree than any other agricultural product. Encouraged by Virginia's prosperity,

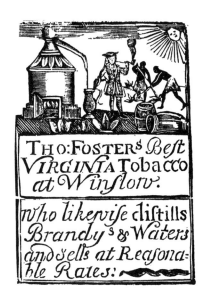

Tobacco labels, c. 1700, promoted drinking spirits as a companion activity to pipe smoking.
New York Public Library

farmers in the colonies of Maryland, New Netherlands, New Sweden, and Massachusetts were eager to try their hands at growing tobacco, too.

By the end of the seventeenth century tobacco was king not only in Virginia but also throughout the North American colonies and in Europe, where it had been introduced to the royal court of France by the French ambassador to Portugal. It was this statesman and scientist, Jean Nicot, who identified the component of tobacco that scholars named after him: nicotine.

With pipes being smoked everywhere, Raleigh's early prediction as he lit his first pipe that he was lighting a candle that would never be extinguished appeared to have come true. The poet Sir Samuel Garth (1660–1718) wrote:

> *Hail! social pipe–thou foe of care,*
> *Companion of my elbow-chair;*
> *As forth thy curling fumes arise,*
> *They seem an evening sacrifice—*
> *An offering to my Maker's praise,*
> *For all His benefits and grace.*

2

O Blessed Pipe

O blessed pipe,
That now I clutch with my gripe,
What joy is in thy smooth, round bowl,
As black as coal!

—ANDREW WYNTER
"Ode to My Pipe"

*T*he Bible specifies that God created the heavens and the earth. It goes on to relate other beginnings, from the first man and woman to the first sin, followed in short order by the invention of clothing, the eviction of the tenants of the Garden of Eden by an angry landlord, and the first murder. Scripture also indicates that wine was most likely the invention of the world's first vintner, Noah, who also became history's first zookeeper.

Although many of the world's religions incorporated burning incense into their rituals, nowhere in the long saga of relations between deities and human beings, and the world we were given, is there an answer as to why, how, where, and when we began setting fire to dried leaves of certain plants and finding pleasure in drawing the smoke through a tube into our mouths.

To find the origins of pipe smoking we have to turn instead to the archaeologists. What their numerous diggings tell us is that the pipe was being used in Europe before the adventuresome sailors of Spain, England, and France set foot in the Americas. The Celtic people of Ireland, in addition to inventing whiskey, smoked aromatic herbs in iron pipes long before Columbus set his compass westward in hopes of finding a shorter route to the treasures of the Orient, only to stumble onto the lands of the Western Hemisphere. Farther back in time, an artist created a fresco in the Roman city of Pompeii depicting a group of men playing a game called Knucklebone in which one of the figures is smoking a pipe. What he had in it, and what the Irish were smoking before Columbus embarked, is anybody's guess. But it definitely wasn't tobacco.

Pompeii had been long since buried in ashes of the volcano Vesuvius before Europeans observed the natives of the New World smoking the leaves of a plant found only in the Americas. They had been doing so for many thousands of years. The evidence was unearthed in burial mounds in North America in the form of stone and earthen pipes. A carving in a Mayan temple in Mexico that has been dated to the first century A.D. depicts a priest in elaborate ceremonial costume puffing on a long, straight pipe. In 1512 the Spanish explorer Ponce de Leon found pipes in use in Florida. But it was not until the French explorer Jacques Cartier ventured into Canada (1535–1536) that Europeans were given a detailed description of pipe smoking by native Americans:

> There groweth a certain kind of Herb, whereof in Summer they make great provision for all the year, and first they cause it to be dried in the Sun, then wear around their neck in a little bag, with a hollow piece of stone or wood like a pipe [note: this refers to the musical instrument]. Then when they please they make a powder of it, and then put it into one of the ends, and laying a coal of fire upon it at the other end suck so long, that they fill their bod-ies full of smoke, till it comes out of their mouth and nostrils. They say that this does keep them warm and in health. They never go without some of it about them. We ourselves have tried the same smoke, and having put it in our mouths, it seemed that they had filled it with Pepper dust, it is so hot.

Cartier's countrymen came up with a term for the pipe of the American Indians, derived from the Latin *calamus* and Old French *chalemel,* meaning "reed."

The Calumet

The pipe as we know it today is traceable to the religious cere-monial Indian pipe that the French called "calumet," and that has been depicted in countless Hollywood movies about the American West as "the peace pipe."

Sixteenth-century pen and ink drawing of a Native American Indian smoking a calumet (peace pipe).
New York Public Library

One religious ritual involving the calumet was described in 1972 in *Black Elk Speaks: Being the Life Story of a Holy Man of Oglala Sioux,* by John G. Neihardt. The rite was known as "The Offering of the Pipe."

Now I light the pipe, and after I have offered it to the powers that are one Power, and sent forth a voice to them, we shall smoke together. Offering the mouthpiece first of all to the One above—so—I send a voice:

Hey hey! hey hey! hey hey! hey hey!

This is my prayer; hear me! The voice I have sent is weak, yet with earnestness I have sent it. Hear me!

It is finished. *Hetchetu Aloh!*

Now, my friend, let us smoke together so that there may be only good between us!

In writing about Indian pipe rituals in *The Pipe Smoker* (1980), John Paul Beaumier and Lewis Camp said, "In many senses, the sacred pipe of the Indians is the most ingenious religious artifact ever invented. It is not the smoke itself that alone suffices. It depends on what the smoke is made of. In every case it must be the fumy essence of something so precious that the gods will accept the offering."

Universally among American Indians that precious and divine substance was tobacco, and the instrument by which the gift to the gods was offered skyward, and to the four winds, in the form of smoke was the calumet. But there was important symbolism in the pipe itself as well. It provided not only a chalice for the tobacco, but also a tangible emblem of the contract being made between those who smoked it, and of their mutual recognition that they smoked it in the presence of a supernatural power.

Engraving of a tobacco plant and Native American Indian with a calumet, 1738.
New York Public Library

The calumet bowl was made of wood, as was the stem. Long and straight, it represented honesty and sincerity. It was commonly decorated with beads and animal hide. Feathers could be added—white for peace, red for war.

Pipes of Indians of the Great Plains were also made from a red stone found in Minnesota. Easily carved when first taken from the ground, it hardens quickly in air. This material came to be known as

Stone pipes from Baffin Land, Hudson's Bay.
New York Public Library

pipestone; the area from which it was taken was called "Fountain of the Pipe."

Although located in territory of the Sioux, the region was regarded as neutral ground by all Indian tribes. Following the appearance in the area in 1841 of the artist and writer George Catlin, who published two volumes that contained four hundred engraved illustrations of Indian life, pipestone was given the name catlinite. It is still quarried to make pipe bowls.

Furnace with Tube

The French had another word for the tobacco pipe. Because the bowl resembled a furnace, the dictionary *Larousse* listed it as *fourneau* and described it as a furnace with a tube attached. A treatise on smoking published in France in 1845 still made the comparison. It defined a pipe as "a tube, more or less long, of various shapes, connected with a furnace, through which one draws into the mouth tobacco smoke."

Soldiers in the French Grande Armée took to calling a pipe a *bouffard*. This was in tribute to Corporal Jean Nepoma Bouffardi. After he had lost both arms in a battle, one of them was found with a pipe still clutched in the hand. His compatriots kept the pipe and venerated it as symbol of their regiment.

In England Dr. Samuel Johnson's "great dictionary" said a tobacco pipe was "a tube of clay through which the fume of tobacco is drawn into the mouth."

That *pipe* in connection with tobacco smoking required definition was because the word had been in use for centuries to describe objects that held liquids. Example: a pipe of wine. Some scholars on the origin of words cite the Latin *pipa,* meaning "hollow reed." Its use in this manner appears in a rite of Christians of the Byzantine Empire, who used a tube of gold to draw wine from the chalice in the Sacrament of Communion *(pipa ad surgendum vinum calici).*

In Old High German the pipe was *phifa* or *pfeiffe.*

For Danes it became *pibe.*

The Welsh and Irish made it *pib.*

In the movie version of Agatha Christie's novel *Murder on the Orient Express,* when Albert Finney as the Belgian-born private detective Hercule Poirot pronounced it "peep," Sean Connery made a point of correcting him by emphasizing that he smoked a *pipe.*

From the day a pipe was first placed into the eager hands of Sir Walter Raleigh, the English brushed aside any possibility of confusion with water pipes, bagpipes, flutes, or other musical instruments and took the device used in smoking tobacco to their hearts as a pipe. As early as 1606 a character in a play declared the tobacco pipe "the gentleman's saint and the soldier's idol."

Despite oppressions laid upon smokers by King James, there was a Society of Tobacco-pipe-makers with a coat of arms that pictured a tobacco plant in full bloom. The society's motto was "Let brotherly love continue." The sentiment and the making of pipes outlived James, who died in 1625 knowing not only that his efforts to crush tobacco smoking had failed miserably, but indeed, on the day of his demise

Tobacco labels used by British tobacconists in 1675.
New York Public Library

there were more tobacco shops in London than alehouses and taverns. (Raleigh's severed head must have been chuckling with delight.)

Pipe makers boldly proclaimed their craft by embossing their handiwork with their initials. One contemporary observer wrote, "Monograms and designs were stamped or moulded upon the bowls and on the stems." In one of those ironic twists that appear to be endemic in history, many of these "signature" pipes of the latter half of the seventeenth century were presented by English colonists to Indians, sometimes as peace offerings but frequently as payment for Indian real estate. In 1677 more than one hundred were given for a strip of land near Timber Creek, New Jersey. And the founder of Pennsylvania, William Penn, bought a huge tract of land from the natives for three hundred pipes and assorted other articles.

Although Penn was not a smoker, late-seventeenth-century English "tobacconists," as they were known at the time (meaning tobacco smokers, not sellers) included Sir Isaac Newton, of theory-of-gravity fame; Thomas Hobbes, philosopher; poet-physician Sir Samuel Garth; and Izaak Walton, although smoking was not mentioned in his *Compleat Angler.*

Whether called pipes by these Englishmen and their colonial cousins in America, the "furnaces" of the French, the Germans' *pfeiffe,* the *pibe* of Denmark, or the *pib* of the Welsh and Irish, these little bowls of burning tobacco at the tip of a long or a short stem for sucking out the smoke had one thing in common:

They were all made of the same stuff.

The Old Clay Pipe

One fine autumn day in England in 1598 an amiable foreigner by the name of Paul Hentzler dropped in at the Southwark Bear Garden, a kind of combination zoo-circus. But it wasn't the animals that fascinated him. He found the Englishmen much more interesting, so much so that he wrote, "At these spectacles and everywhere else the English are constantly smoking tobacco in this manner: They have pipes on purpose made of clay, into the further end of which they put the herb, so dry that it may be rubbed into powder, and putting fire to it they draw the smoke into their mouths, which they puff out again through their nostrils, like funnels."

In 1615 another observer wrote (disapprovingly) of Englishmen who "from wantonness [and] with an insatiable desire and greediness suck in the stinking smoke through an earthen pipe, which presently they blow out again through their nostrils, insomuch that tobacco shops are now as ordinary as taverns and taphouses."

The earthen pipes observed by both men were made of a white clay that was kneaded, shaped, and placed unwashed into an oven to be baked like pottery. The earliest forms had been copied from the pipes smoked by American Indians, but their small, shallow cups soon proved insufficient in size to satisfy the appetites of the Europeans who avidly took up tobacco smoking. Consequently, pipe makers in England altered the dimensions of the bowl to form a kind of barrel, which could accommodate a larger load of tobacco. They also gave the bowl a forward tilt and, for convenience when setting down the pipe in order to quaff a little ale, a flattened bottom. The stems ran from four to six inches in length.

As smoking caught on and became widespread, and as more tobacco became available from Virginia, the pipe makers enlarged the bowls and lengthened the stems. Because these bigger bowls became very hot, the flat bottom was eliminated in favor of a spur held between thumb and forefinger that served as a handle. By the close of the seventeenth century the bowls were about half an inch in diameter and more elongated. Eventually, as pipe makers got better at their

Illustration by H. Brown in De Nederland, *published in 1841, shows a "kolf-player" holding a long clay pipe cross-wise in his mouth.* New York Public Library

craft, clay pipes took on smoother finishes, grew less brittle, and became more graceful in appearance.

"These pipes showed a very high standard of skill by the mould-makers," wrote Eric G. Ayto in *Clay Tobacco Pipes.* Some pipe makers in London made pipes with heraldic arms and Masonic and other emblems. Public houses (pubs) offered customers clay pipes bearing the establishments' names. Military regiments wanted pipes bearing their insignia.

Extra-long pipes—their stems ran eighteen to twenty-four inches—made for the gentry became known as aldermen. It was a style that stayed in fashion well into the nineteenth century. Around 1850 an even lengthier version had a rather brief vogue. Its stem was thirty-six inches long and was known, not surprisingly, as "a yard of clay."

To assist the smoker in handling this mammoth pipe the makers attached a label at the point of balance. Later in the century another style of gigantic pipe was employed during sermons to poke parishioners who dozed off. These became known derisively, particularly in the writings of Charles Dickens, as churchwardens.

Between Sundays, the common man went about his daily life and labors smoking stubby clays. Because they were cut short they were called "cutty pipes." Examples of them unearthed by the thousands in archaeological digs in Ireland were also known as "Danish," "fairy," and "elfin pipes." Tobacco had been regarded as a medicine capable of warding off the plague, so these were used by the masses and found in graves of victims of the "black death." This use earned the small pipes the macabre sobriquet of "plague pipes."

By the time of the ascension of Queen Victoria to the throne of England (1837), the workmanship of some clay pipes had reached the level of art. Especially proud smokers who had the financial wherewithal ordered clay pipes sculpted into portraits of themselves. Famous personalities—actors, comedians, jockeys—found themselves immortalized on clay pipe bowls. But for most smokers the pipe of choice was the unadorned, short-stemmed version described in a contemporary poem by A. B. Van Fleet. The first stanza of "My Old Clay Pipe" went:

> There's a lot of solid comfort
>   In an old clay pipe, I find,
> If you're kind of out of humor
>   Or in trouble in your mind.
> When you're feeling awful lonesome
>   And don't know what to do,
> There's a heap of satisfaction
>   If you smoke a pipe or two.

By the third decade of Queen Victoria's reign, however, the era of the fragile "old clay" was drawing to its close. A new style of pipe manufactured from a sturdier material and promising smokers many years of reliable pleasure was at hand.

The Briar

According to the Old Testamant, when God booted Adam and Eve out of the Garden of Eden they were advised in no uncertain terms that from then on they were on their own. No more heavenly freebies. A house? Build it yourself. Food? Plant seeds and harvest them. Clothing? Well, the couple had already demonstrated a knack for covering their nakedness, so it was bound to be only a matter of time until some descendants of Adam and Eve would become high-fashion models parading down the runways of the haute couture salons of New York and Paris.

Whether humanity emerged from the biblical Garden of Eden or out of a patch of hardscrabble land in what we call Africa (as the evolutionists would have it), if history has proved anything since the day our ancestors set out to tame the world it's that our astonishing capacity for making things is surpassed only by our urge to mess around with something someone else has made in hopes of improving it. You could say that our entire history is perfectly captured in the old maxim, "Build a better mousetrap and the world will beat a path to your door."

So it was as inevitable as tomorrow's sunrise that someone would tinker with the pipe. As delightful as the clay pipe was, it had a lot of shortcomings. It was fragile: Drop one and it shattered, and there went your bowl of tobacco. The stems broke. Sooner or later, what with all the charring, bowls cracked. Most irksome was that after a while clays got to be too hot to handle.

As in almost all the "firsts" of history, there are different versions regarding precisely whose brainstorm resulted in the wooden pipe replacing the clay as the preferred smoking device. We do know that American Indians used pipes made of wood, but it was not until the middle of the eighteenth century that a written reference can be found regarding a European smoking a wooden pipe.

On March 18, 1765, Tobias Smollett wrote a letter saying that while journeying from Nice, France, to Turin, Italy, he had reached the top of "the mountain Brovis" and met a very tall, meager, and yellow man with a long, hooked nose and twinkling eyes wearing a woolen nightcap, over which he wore a floppy hat. Around his neck was a silk handkerchief. But the feature of more interest to Smollett than the clothing of this quixotic figure was the nature of the pipe he held clenched in his teeth. It was a short *wooden* pipe. Smollett recorded that the man turned out to be an Italian marquis, but recorded nothing further about the pipe, such as where the marquis had acquired it and from whom.

The next written record of wooden pipes in Europe is the word of one A. J. Munby, who claimed in 1853 that he had helped introduce wooden pipes into England. He wrote that "a college friend of mine, a Norfolk squire, possessed a gardener who was of an inventive turn [who] conceived and wrought out the idea of making pipes of willow-wood, cutting the bowl out of a thick stem, and the tube out of a thinner one growing from the bowl, so that the whole pipe was of one piece."

Unfortunately, the name of that gardener was not provided— although even if it had been recorded, it probably would have become a mere footnote in the history of pipes. Willow wood proved too soft to make a durable pipe.

Another European candidate for the distinction of introducing a pipe made of wood is a French pipe maker who in the mid-1850s set off on a pilgrimage to the birthplace of Napoleon on the island of Corsica. When his pipe broke, he commissioned a peasant to carve a pipe from a local wood that was notable for its hardness and fine grain. With a cry of *"Tout à fait magnifique,"* the pilgrim asked the name of the wood.

The French name, it turned out, is *bruyère,* derived from the Low Latin *brugaria,* which was a twist by the ancient Romans on the Celtic word for bush, *brug.* One such bush was actually the dwarflike, robust heath tree. With wide-spreading roots, it *(Erica arborea)* is found in Corsica, Sardinia, Italy, elsewhere around the Mediterranean, and France. There are two varieties, the *bruyère blanche* (white heath) and *bruyère mauve* (purple). It is the root of the white that proved ideal for making handsome, fairly inexpensive, easy-smoking, but hard and tough pipes. Made mostly in the region of Saint-Claude in France, they were to flood into England and send the clay pipe into virtual oblivion.

"The briar pipe not only soon drove the clay largely out of use," G. L. Apperson wrote in *The Social History of Smoking* (1916), "but it immensely increased the number of pipe smokers."

A World of Pipes

While the briar pipe was capturing the fancy of the pipe smokers of Victorian England, the men who took the queen's shilling and went to sea in the ships of the Royal Navy were creating an empire upon which, it was said, the sun never set. And in this era in which Britannia ruled the waves, the sailors put into foreign ports where Sir Walter Raleigh's tobacco was being smoked in pipes as varied as the people and the customs of the lands themselves.

A British "tar" taking shore leave during a friendly visit to Germany, where the Kaiser was a relative of Victoria—as were most of the monarchs of Europe—could find Germans puffing away on wooden pipes with big bowls elaborately carved with Teutonic designs featuring stags, wild boars, and forest scenes. Some of these had a hinged lid to keep out wind and rain; others were made with porcelain-lined bowls (as were some pipes in England).

In countries of North Africa, where society and custom had been shaped by the Islamic religion of the Moors and Arabs, the pipe was a combination of wood and clay. Known as the *adham* (Arabic for bone) or the *touba,* it was short and straight and resembled a small leg or arm bone. The mouth of the bowl faced forward rather than upward. Capable of containing only a tiny amount of tobacco, it provided the smoker barely five or six puffs.

In the marketplaces of the exotic cities in the Middle East (called the Near East by the Victorians), the locals favored the water pipe. Known as the hookah, it was a jar (large or small) filled from one-half to three-quarters with water and sealed with a stopper. Extending nearly to the bottom of the jar was a tube that was connected at the top to the bowl. Another tube was flexible and fitted with a mouthpiece. Sucking on this drew the smoke into the jar, through the water,

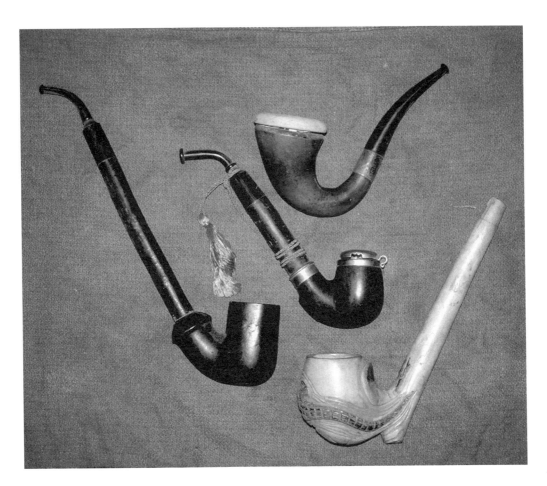

A sampling of old pipes, including one with a hinged lid to keep out wind and rain.
© Kevin Gordon

up again through the flexible tube, and into the mouth. (A century later in the United States and elsewhere the water pipe would be adopted as a means of smoking marijuana.)

Were an English sailor to encounter a traveling Frenchman he might see him puffing a *gambier.* A clay pipe named after its inventor, this usually had a cherrywood stem and ebonite mouthpiece.

Turks had a pipe called a *chibouk.* It had a bell-shaped bowl made of red clay and a long stem of jasmine or cherrywood that ended in a slightly curved mouthpiece made of amber, bone, or tortoise shell. Turks and other Asians also smoked from a *narghile.* Similar to a water pipe, it had a bowl at the top of a long tube that ended in a small water container. A flexible tube extended from it to the mouth.

Turkey also provided the pipe-smoking world with a unique substance that German pipe makers named meerschaum and the French called *écume de mer.* The terms mean "sea surf." A hydrous silicate of magnesia found by the seaside, it was boiled in milk then kneaded with linseed oil and wax to form a lump of clay. This was cut into blocks and shaped by turning into roughly shaped bowls. Rubbing, polishing, waxing, and glazing produce a lightweight pipe of considerable luxury. Its virtues as a pipe, as well as its beauty, are only enhanced by repeated smoking.

While Queen Victoria's seafaring subjects encountered all these kinds of pipes as they and their ships held Victoria's empire together, it was in the only colonies to break away from British rule that the incidence of pipe smoking surpassed the passion of the English for tobacco.

The Pipe in the United States

Sooner or later (presumably), every student in history classes in the United States learns that citizens of the colony of Massachusetts protested the imposition of taxes by the government of England on tea by having a party in Boston in 1773. The festivities consisted of heaving crates of tea into Boston Harbor. Less known was a nonviolent event of similar portent that took place two years later in Virginia.

Since 1662 clergymen had been paid in tobacco. But as the result of a drought that inflated this product's value, the Virginia legislature passed an act requiring the churchmen to be paid in currency. This entailed a sharp decline in the living standards of men of the cloth. Then the Privy Council, the executive arm of the British Crown, struck down the law. Consequently, while the law had been in effect the ministers had been *underpaid*.

When the Reverend James Maury of Hanovor County sued for back wages in a case known as the Parson's Cause, he engaged as his advocate a brilliant young lawyer with a talent for incendiary language. Patrick Henry argued in court that when the Privy Council threw out the currency-compensation law, the King of England had broken the compact between ruler and governed, forfeiting "all rights to his subjects' obedience." The court found in favor of the minister, only to see its verdict thrown out by the Privy Council. As a drumroll for American independence spread throughout the English colonies, Henry went on to assert, "As for me, give me liberty or death."

When words failed to achieve independence and Americans took up guns to fight for it, Benjamin Franklin set aside his pipe for a moment to propose that one way to help pay for the cost of the war was to slap a tax on tobacco sales.

Like most of the gentlemen farmers of eighteenth-century Virginia who became leaders in the struggle for independence, Patrick Henry raised tobacco. Among the others was George Washington, who regularly shipped his product to England in large quantities known as hogsheads. These were the "roles" mentioned by Raleigh in noting how the remainder of a shipload of tobacco to Plymouth had been divvied up among the ship's admiral, a friend, and himself.

Although Sir Walter used the Old English spelling—roles—hogsheads were immense bundles of tobacco pressed and bound into cylinders after the leaves had been harvested, cleaned of stems, and cured. Each hogshead was then rolled out of the barn onto a road, where a spike was driven into each side of it. To these were attached shafts that in turn were hitched to a pair of horses. With a driver astride the rear horse the hogshead rolled away like a wagon to its destination, sometimes to a stream or river to be loaded on a barge for shipment to a merchant in a city, or sometimes directly to a port for shipment overseas.

One of the first merchants to receive Virginia tobacco had his business on Chatham Street—"near the jail," as an early advertisement pointed out—in New York City. He was a French immigrant, Pierre Lorillard, who along with his sons, Peter and George, built his small enterprise into one of the great tobacco firms in American history. Among the company's firsts was the use of waterpower (the Bronx River) to run a tobacco mill (it is now part of the New York Botanical Garden). Lorillard also pioneered tobacco advertising in newspapers (1787) and nationwide distribution of manufatured tobacco merchandise when U.S. postmasters agreed to allow Lorillard products be sold through the mail in 1830. Using a "tin tag," the firm achieved the first effective trademarking of tobacco products in 1860. The company's pipe tobacco was sold under the brand names Union Leader, Friends, India House, and Briggs until 1973, when Lorillard divested its manufacturing and marketing of pipe tobaccos to concentrate on cigarettes.

From the days of John Rolfe through the eighteenth century and right up to the Civil War, most of the tobacco sold by men like Lorillard was for use in pipes. Their supremacy would continue until the invention of machinery that enabled tobacconists to mass-produce and mass-market inexpensive cigars, beginning in the 1880s. At that time the pipe being smoked in England and elsewhere was the clay. But in 1868 a new and uniquely American kind of pipe made its commercial debut.

The Corncob

Although the natives of North America were known to smoke pipes made from corncobs, credit for formally introducing them on a commercial scale belongs to a Dutch settler, Henry Tibbe, who founded a company bearing his name in 1868. He later changed the name to The Missouri Meerschaum Company. It is still the main maker of corncobs—by hand, one pipe at a time (thirty-five thousand a year), in the same brick building on which Tibbe first hung out his shingle.

A woodcarver by trade, Tibbe engaged a local druggist to whip up a plaster-of-paris paste in which he soaked the porous cobs in order to seal them. This overcame the chief drawback of corncobs: They smoked hot and wet. To give the Missouri Meerschaums a classier look Tibbe sanded the exteriors, giving them a smooth-to-the-touch feel. On their first day of sale at a nickel apiece, Tibbe's entire stock quickly disappeared.

One of the corncob's most ardent smokers was Daniel Boone. A fellow Tennessee frontiersman who smoked a corncob was Davy Crockett, who died a hero at the Alamo, as did his comrade in arms, Jim Bowie.

Others who fancied corncob pipes included Samuel Langhorne Clemens (Mark Twain), who hired someone to break his in; World War I general John J. "Black Jack" Pershing; and, arguably the most famous and visible of the military corncob smokers, General Douglas MacArthur.

The Pipe between the Wars

The period from the end of the Civil War to the turn of the century saw a growth in regional agricultural specialization. The north-central states accounted for almost half the wheat, half the barley, and nearly all the flaxseed grown. The mountain states dominated the wool market. Oats were the thing in Illinois and Iowa, where Quaker Oats put down roots to provide Americans with packaged oatmeal and, later, puffed wheat and rice—although rice was the chief agricultural product of Louisiana, accounting for 70 percent of the national output. Major sources of milk for a bowl of breakfast cereal were Iowa, Illinois, New York, and Wisconsin, which also carved out the leadership role in making cheese. For its tobacco America continued to look primarily to Virginia, along with North Carolina, Tennessee, and Kentucky.

To purchase tobacco and a pipe to put it in, the smoker in the years between the Civil War and World War I did not simply go into town, or downtown, on a Saturday afternoon to find a pipe shop. These did not exist as such; indeed, the first "pipe stores" did not open their doors until about 1910. The emporium where a man bought a Missouri Meerschaum or briar, along with the tobacco to fill it, was either a general store or a shop with a wooden figure of an Indian in front advertising cigars, for by the close of the nineteenth century America's smokers had taken the stogie into their hearts and mouths.

World War II's General Douglas MacArthur was introduced to the corncob pipe by the top commander of American forces in World War I, General John J. "Black Jack" Pershing, a native of Missouri.
Missouri Meerschaum Company

Taking up cigar smoking at that time made sense for various reasons. Invention of cigar-rolling machinery in the 1880s permitted mass-production. This made cigars cheaper. With so much product to sell, cigar makers turned to advertising on a national scale. Consequently, smokers who encountered these ads for low-cost cigars learned that cigar smoking could be not only a cheaper way to enjoy tobacco, but also far less cumbersome and demanding of attention than the pipe.

In 1890 more than four billion cigars were sold in the United States. Sixteen years later sales had almost doubled. In 1904 cigar sales accounted for sixty cents of the dollar available for tobacco. About a third of this dollar went for pipe smoking; only a nickel was spent on cigarettes. The paper-wrapped little tubes of tobacco would, however, begin making inroads into the tobacco market in the next decade, for the same reasons as the rise in popularity of cigars.

Pipe smoking had declined in favor of the cigar and cigarette to such an extent by 1913 that a newspaper in England ran an article titled "A Plea for the Pipe." The author asked "pipe-men of all degrees" if the time had not "really arrived to enter a protest against the convention which forces the pipe into a position of inferiority, and exalts to a pinnacle of undeserved pre-eminence the cigar, and still more the cigarette?"

The dominance of the pipe in the world of American smokers suffered another setback with the outbreak of world war in 1914. Importation of pipes became very difficult, if not impossible. And when the "doughboy" went "Over There," to the tune of George M. Cohan's patriotic song, there was little room in his old kit bag for pipes and tins of tobacco. It was a whole lot easier to carry a box of "lucifers" (matches) to light up a "fag," as the English called their cigarettes.

Returning soldiers who soon found themselves caught in the frenzied frolics of the "Roaring Twenties" discovered that the cigarette was all the rage. Women were also smoking them, and in public, while flaunting federal laws outlawing the sale and distribution of alcoholic beverages by downing booze in speakeasies and at cocktail parties. These were hardly the right spots to light up and casually smoke a pipe. The delight of Raleigh and those who followed him in pipe smoking was, as the nineteenth-century English novelist William Makepeace Thackeray had observed, a way of smoking that "generates a style of conversation, contemplative, thoughtful, benevolent and unaffected."

Like the general history of the United States through the twentieth century, the smoking of pipes has had its high points and low. It was up during the Great Depression, down again in World War II, and back up in the postwar period, only to decline in the next three decades, due in some respects to an anti-smoking movement at least as virulent as that of King James I.

While cigarette smoking would continue to win converts, far surpassing both pipes and cigars in sales, there persisted in the first half of the twentieth century a significant core of devotees to Raleigh's

My Friendly Pipe

Let sybarites still dream delights
    While smoking cigarettes,
Whose opiates get in their pates
    Till waking brings regrets;
Oh, let them doze, devoid of woes,
    Of troubles and of frets.
And let the chap who loves to nap
    With his cigar in hand
Pursue his way, and live his day,
    As runs time's changing sand;
Let him delight by day and nights
    In his peculiar brand.
But as for me, I love to be
    Provided with a pipe,—
A rare old bowl to warm my soul,
    A meerschaum brown and ripe,—
With good plug cut, no stump or butt,
    Nor filthy gutter-snipe.
My joys increase! It brings me peace
    As nothing else can do;
From all the strife of life
    Here my relief is true
I watch its rings; it purrs and sings—
    And then it's cheaper, too!
                    —*Detroit Tribune,* 1895

way of smoking tobacco and aficionados of Columbus's discovery. This period also witnessed improvements in the production of both varieties, helping make the United States the largest market in the world for both pipes and cigars.

World events also contributed to a generally steady popularity for the pipe. As Richard Carleton Hacker noted in *The Ultimate Pipe Book,* published in 1984, "the world, with its newfound knowledge of the atomic bomb and synthetic materials, became a more sobering place to live, and man began searching for remnants of the old values, symbols of shady tree-lined streets and cozy brick homes with fireplaces."

With more than twenty million pipe smokers in America, Hacker pointed out, the pipe still provides an image of stability that remains a bastion of individuality.

3

The Gentlemanly Smoke

When love grows cool, the fire still warms me;
When friends are fled, thy presence charms me.
If thou art full, though purse be bare,
I smoke, and cast away all care!

—GERMAN SMOKING SONG

S herlock Holmes was thinking.

He sat coiled in his armchair, his haggard and ascetic face hardly visible among the blue swirl of his tobacco smoke, his black brows down, his forehead contracted, his eyes vacant and far away. Finally, he laid down his pipe, sprang to his feet, and declared, "It won't do, Watson!"

With this glimpse of the sleuth of 221B Baker Street in "The Devil's Foot," published in *Strand* magazine in London in December 1910, Arthur Conan Doyle in the words of Dr. John H. Watson presented his pipe-smoking detective as a Victorian gentleman of intelligence, studiousness, and independence of mind. Content to be solitary and sedentary, he was nonetheless ready, if called for, to plunge into decisive motion. Often after an evening spent in rooms he shared with Watson, filling the suite with tobacco fumes generated as he pondered the complexities of a "three pipe problem," he would roust the good doctor from his slumber with the cry to action, "The game's afoot."

It is this image of Sherlock Holmes as "a reasoning machine" mulling the intricacies of a puzzle with life itself at stake that promoted in people's minds the persistent stereotype of the pipe smoker as brainy.

In cinematic history, along with Sherlock Holmes as played by numerous actors, the portrait of the pipe smoker was Fred MacMurray or Spencer Tracy. For film fans of a later generation he was Denholm Elliott as the soft-spoken, bemused sidekick of Harrison Ford in the *Indiana Jones* series.

In the comic strips he is Dennis the Menace's father.

In everybody's experience he is at least one teacher in high school, a college prof, or a favorite uncle.

This image of the pipe smoker as erudite gentleman began in Sir Walter Raleigh's day when the pipe was taken up by Elizabeth I's courtiers, to be followed by an intellectual elite that to this day includes writers, philosophers, educators, doctors, lawyers, and scientists. The latter group included nearly all the brainy men who invented the atomic bomb, from Albert Einstein, Enrico Fermi, Robert Oppenheimer, and Edward Teller (who also built the hydrogen bomb) to Leslie Groves, the no-nonsense army general who proved himself a quick learner of the destructive uses of nuclear physics as the man in charge of the Manhattan Project.

But science of a different and more benign quality was used by Burton Shean to test the validity of the stereotypical view of the pipe smoker as an intellectual. The results of his survey were reported in an article, "The Pipe Wears Many Hats," in the magazine *Wonderful World of Pipes.*

Smokers of cigarettes and those who smoked tobacco in pipes had been given two sets of questions. The first group asked:

- Do you prefer taking action over planning action?

- Do you rate yourself as a lively individual?

- Are you happiest taking part in something that calls for rapid action?

- Are you usually inclined to be quick and sure in your actions?

- Do you take the initiative in making new friends?

- Would you be unhappy if you were prevented from making numerous social contacts?

The second set asked:

- Do you become so absorbed in whatever you are doing that you don't welcome being interrupted?

- Do you remain outwardly calm when those around you become excited?

- Do you prefer the familiar to taking chances with the new and untried?

Cigarette smokers generally answered yes to the first set. Pipe smokers were affirmative regarding the second.

Shean's study concluded that the traditional image of the pipe man as contemplative, solid, and careful in thinking is in some measure true. It's the picture of a mature gentleman wearing a tweed jacket with leather elbow patches, seated comfortably in a red leather wing chair in a book-lined room with a fire crackling, half-moon reading glasses resting on the tip of his nose, and a book opened in his lap.

In *The Pipe Smoker,* Beaumier and Camp noted that the pipe smoker has always been special. They wrote, "He does not often blush or show anxiety; rather, he seems cool, deliberate, patient, and contemplative. He is perceived as thoughtful and kindly, a man who can be trusted."

To support these conclusions the authors cited another survey, conducted in 1973. It examined the social image of the pipe smoker.

The Criswell Survey

In setting out to evaluate the popular picture of the pipe smoker, Eleanor Criswell conducted individual interviews and group consultations to discern what that popular image was. She talked to both smokers and nonsmokers and found them in accord as to which adjectives apply to pipe smokers: *stable, masculine, calm, pensive, collegiate, professorial, distinguished-looking, conservative in dress, tweedy, staid, aloof, internalized,* and sometimes *absent-minded.* In all, the poll resulted in 104 ways to characterize the pipe smoker.

Using these terms as the basis for a questionnaire, Criswell then surveyed two thousand people, half of them pipe-smoking men and the other half women who knew men who smoked pipes. Around 40 percent of the men responded, and a little more than a third of the women. Roughly 90 percent of all respondents agreed with the 104 adjectives. And the same percentage of women added their own descriptions, including *strong, reliable, good-natured, self-controlled, considerate, conscientious, not at all shy or absent-minded, affectionate, handsome,* and *sexy.*

The Immortality of the Pipe

"What is more delightful," asked Carl Weber in his book *The Pleasures of Pipe Smoking* (1965), "than to sit with a rich and delicately-veined pipe before a fireplace in which fragrant wood is burning, and spin yarns of high adventure in far-off places? Or, when the company is intimate, to sit and smoke in silence—with only the hiss and pop of the logs to punctuate one's thoughts?"

The moment a man takes a pipe he becomes a philosopher, said Thomas Chandler Haliburton in "Sam Slick" in 1836. "It's the poor man's friend; it calms the mind, soothes the temper, and makes a man patient under difficulties. It has made more good men, good husbands, kind masters, indulgent fathers, than any other thing on this blessed earth."

Three years later in London, *A Paper on Tobacco* observed, "How soothing is a pipe to the wearied sportsman on his return to the inn from the moors! As he sits quietly smoking, he thinks of his absent friends in a perfect state of contentment with himself and the world."

And as noted earlier, Thackeray believed a pipe draws wisdom from the lips of the philosopher and shuts up the foolish.

But couldn't this be said about all kinds of smoking? What is it about a pipe that separates it from cigarettes and cigars?

G. L. Apperson proposed in *The Social History of Smoking* that the pipe is the most satisfactory of smokes because a man *owns* a pipe. "A cigar or a cigarette is—and it is not," he wrote, but "the pipe renders its service again and again."

This is true. Cigarettes or cigars are chosen on the basis of status as signified by brand or, perhaps, entirely because of price. But when a cigarette or cigar has been smoked, it and its "pedigree" are gone—used up—and its remnants discarded.

With a pipe it's only the tobacco that's consumed. The pipe is still yours. It remains as an expression of everything about you, as surely as the clothes you choose to wear, your style of shoes, your necktie, your cologne or aftershave lotion, the cut of your hair (or lack of it), and whether you hold your pants up with belt or braces.

Cigarette advertising notwithstanding, no one has ever been defined by the brand of cigarette he smokes. The package may bear a fancy or even an elegant name, but the contents are pretty much the same as other brands. While a cigar smoker may contend that much may be known about him by his choice of cigar, this is an illusion. Remove the black-and-gold band of the renowned Cohiba and the prized and costly banned-from-being-imported-to-the-U.S. Havana looks just like any other cigar.

And where is the romance in the crushed and bent carcass of the snuffed-out cigarette or in the corpse of a finished cigar in an ashtray?

A properly cared-for pipe, however, can be your companion to the end of your life. On the day you buy a pipe, you and it begin a journey in which the pipe will become entwined with your experiences; one day these will be called from memory simply by your picking up that pipe. As the nineteenth-century poet John J. Gormley put it:

> You've had your fill of cakes and ale,
>   And half-forgotten memories, too.
>   And all the pensive thoughts that twine
>   Around a past that, entre nous,
>   Has pleasant been, old pipe of mine!

There is also a kind of immortality in a pipe. When you have shuffled off this mortal coil, your pipes will still be there as a part of your estate. They can become cherished reminders of you to those whose lives yours touched and, one would hope, enhanced or even blessed.

But there are other significant differences between cigars or cigarettes and the pipe than transience versus permanence.

The Quiet Man

As Apperson suggested, "Discussions are best conducted over a pipe. No one can get too excited or overheated in argument, no one can neglect the observance of the amenities of conversation [when one] talks thoughtfully between pulls at his pipe [or] has to pause now and again to refill, to strike a light, to knock out the ashes, or to perform one of those numberless little acts of devotion" that go with smoking a pipe.

Certainly, Indians gathered around a campfire and sharing a calumet appreciated this. The pipe, no matter what King James and latter-day foes of smoking may have said (the pipe-smoking tyrant Joseph Stalin notwithstanding), has been a friend of peace, foe of strife, and promoter of geniality and good fellowship. You are not likely to find a pair of pipe smokers erupting into fisticuffs in a tavern.

Rather, as one writer noted, smoking a pipe is a transcendental experience that leaves the mind and body relaxed. In the classic movie *The Quiet Man,* a valentine to Ireland directed by pipe-smoking John Ford, starring pipe smokers John Wayne, Barry Fitzgerald, his brother Arthur Shields, and Victor McLaglen, it takes a great deal of provocation (and a need to bring the story of the film to its denouement) before Wayne (the quiet man of the title) and McLaglen set aside their pipes to settle their affairs. Even the overland brawl that ensues is marked by an atmosphere of mutual respect, and when the battle ends the pair are arm in arm, happily drunk and singing, and certainly harboring no hard feelings.

Countless writers have taken notice of pipe smokers as quiet men and sought to explain the phenomenon. Did a man take up the pipe because he was already a peaceable person? Or did the pipe make him that way?

Thomas Cooper in *Adam Norbrook* thought it was the latter. He wrote, "Now, the pipe calms a man; it slackens his pulse, lulls his restlessness, lays unruly haste and anxiety to sleep, and makes a man willing to stay in the armchair and enjoy it as one of the pleasantest and most comfortable things in life, and let the world, if it will, go a-gadding."

Numerous poets smoked pipes. Did they do so because they were born poets, or did they become poets because they smoked pipes? Few of them did not incorporate into their poetry the pipe and its billowing smoke as a metaphor for life itself, as did this anonymous author:

And when the pipe is out alight
  The smoke ascends, then trembles, wanes,
And soon dissolves in sunshine bright,
  And but the whitened ash remains.
'Tis so man's glory crumble must,
E'en as his body, into dust.

The smoke from a meerschaum, a gift from a friend, captured the fancy of James Russell Lowell:

When curls the smoke in eddies soft,
And hangs a shifting dream aloft,
That gives and takes, though chance-designed,
The impress of the dreamer's mind,
I'll think,—So let the vapors bred
By passion, in the heart or head,
Pass off and upward into space,
Waving farewells of tenderest grace,
Remembered in some happier time,
To blend their beauty with my rhyme.

Another poet, Samuel W. Duffield, wrote of smoking a pipe while playing chess, and found in both a cause to ponder the unanswerable:

And so, as we sat, we reasoned still
Of fate and fortune, of human will,
And what are the purposes men fulfill.

Among countless writers of poetry and prose who smoked pipes were George Gordon, Lord Byron (often in the company of Alfred,

"L'Homme à l'oreille coupée," *a self-portrait by Vincent van Gogh. Van Gogh often included pipes in his paintings.*
New York Public Library

Lord Tennyson), Charles Lamb, Ralph Waldo Emerson, Herman Melville, Rudyard Kipling, Somerset Maugham, James Barrie, Sinclair Lewis, Carl Sandburg, John Steinbeck, Ernest Hemingway, F. Scott Fitzgerald, John O'Hara, J. R. R. Tolkien, Kurt Vonnegut, and Mark Twain.

Painters who smoked pipes range from Vincent van Gogh to Norman Rockwell.

Actors: William Gillette and John Barrymore, both of whom brought portrayals of Sherlock Holmes to the stage in the early years of the twentieth century; Basil Rathbone, whose onscreen Holmes was the definitive Holmes in the 1930s and 1940s, and Jeremy Brett, the inimitable Holmes of the TV screen in the 1980s; Clark Gable; Errol Flynn; William Conrad, radio's Matt Dillon on *Gunsmoke* and TV's *Nero Wolfe* and *Cannon;* Edward G. Robinson, who had the distinction of having both a cigar and a brand of pipe tobacco named after him; James Whitmore, who brought to the stage one-man shows in which he played President Harry S. Truman, Theodore Roosevelt, and Will Rogers before becoming a TV pitchman for garden plant food; and a host of British performers of stage, the silver screen, and television.

On radio, film, and the small screen it would be difficult to imagine anyone more at ease than the popular singer known as "Der Bingle" and "the crooner," and rarely seen without a pipe—Bing Crosby. In the movie *Holiday Inn,* which introduced his and composer Irving Berlin's greatest hit, "White Christmas," Crosby's pipe is much in evidence, including his use of its tip to ring bells on a Christmas tree as he wins the girl away from Fred Astaire in the final scene.

But for the image of the world's most genial fellow one must turn to Clement Moore's "A Visit from St. Nicholas" and the right jolly old elf with the stem of a pipe held tight in his teeth as the smoke encircled his head like a wreath.

Clement Moore's poem "A Visit from St. Nicholas" and this drawing by newspaper cartoonist Thomas Nast created the indelible image of Santa Claus as a "right jolly old elf" smoking a pipe. New York Public Library

One can only imagine Santa Claus home from his whirlwind odyssey around the world, his gift bag empty, the reindeer in their barn, and one of Mrs. Claus's hearty breakfasts settled in his round belly. Nestling into a comfy armchair with his feet up and pipe alit, he is exactly the traditional image of the pipe smoker: a kind, trusty, thoughtful, and happy man relaxing at home after a good day's work.

In his classic book *The Pipe,* published more than half a century ago, Georges Herment wrote, "It can elucidate complexes, soften rancor, appease excitement, solve problems. It gives the system an equilibrium as material as it is spiritual." Thirty years later in *The Ultimate Pipe Book,* Richard Carleton Hacker put it this way: "There is a certain mystique to it all, and, perhaps that is why, when you see someone smoking a pipe, you cannot help but think he knows something you do not."

4

Anatomy of the Pipe

There's clay pipes an' briar pipes
an' meerschaum pipes as well,
There's plain pipes an' fancy pipes. . . .

—HENRY E. BROWN

A pipe is a simple thing, really: a bowl in which to burn tobacco and a connecting tube to draw the resulting smoke into the mouth.

Yet there is much more to it. As Carl Weber noted in *The Pleasures of Pipe Smoking,* these two components may take any imaginable shape and size. They may be long or short, straight or curved, slender or fat. They may offer the haughty beauty of the churchwarden, with its long, clean lines, or arrest the eye with ornate carvings and unusual silhouettes. Indeed, it is difficult to imagine any accessory to one's appearance that is more a mark of individuality than one's choice of pipe.

The selection of a pipe may also provide insight into one's mood, as Dr. Watson pointed out in "The Adventure of the Copper Beeches" when he noted that if Sherlock Holmes set aside a clay for a long cherrywood he was likely to be feeling disputatious rather than meditative. This makes sense. The cherrywood bowl is large and—since it's always made with its original bark intact—conveys a convincing sense of robustness. Because of its rustic and unfinished appearance it has even been described as primitive. It would not be out of line to expect in a moment of intense dispute that a cherrywood smoker might elect to employ his roughly hewn pipe as a weapon—what homicide detectives and coroners call "a blunt instrument."

On the other hand, the pipe most associated with Holmes, the calabash, is so graceful in its shape and light in weight that it is invariably construed as being smoked in placid confines by a gentleman in a velvet smoking jacket with a glass of cognac at hand, his mind immersed in thought and peaceful contemplation. The same may be said of porcelains and delicate meerschaums.

While Holmes turned to cherrywoods, clays, and other kinds of pipes as his moods dictated, the one he smoked more than any other was the one preferred by the majority of pipe smokers for more than a century and a half.

The Briar Pipe

As different as briar pipes appear to the observer in size, shape, and color, and no matter what insights might be garnered from them about the character of the smoker, they have a common anatomy— bowl, stem, mouthpiece.

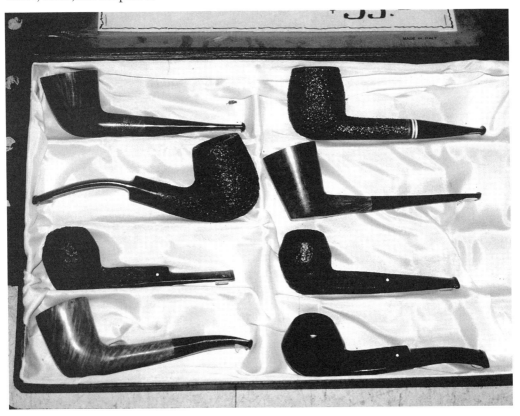

As different as briar pipes appear in size, shape and color, they share a common design—bowl, stem, and mouthpiece.

This design is based on the proposition that tobacco can be burned in a portable device in a way that allows its flavor to be conveyed as smoke without the "furnace" becoming much too hot to handle, and the smoke scorching the mouth. Success in achieving this goal begins with the size, shape, depth, and thickness of the combustion chamber.

THE BOWL

How quickly the tobacco burns is controlled by the width and depth of the bowl. The larger and deeper it is, and the thicker its walls, the cooler the smoke. It consists of the following parts:

Head: The very top of the bowl.

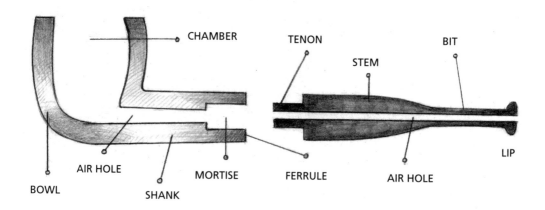

Chamber: The hollowed interior, or furnace, in which the tobacco is packed. The middle contents are known as char. The stuff left at the bottom after a smoke is called dottle.

Foot: The curved base of the bowl containing the airhole. If the hole is in the middle of the bottom of the bowl it is "indirect." If the hole is at the side of the bowl it is "direct."

THE SHANK

An extension of the bowl made of the same block of wood, the shank has an air passage running through it and connects the bowl with the stem. The shank is usually short and either round, square, diamond, or oval in shape. A long shank is known as a Canadian and is usually connected to a short stem or mouthpiece.

Unlike the thickness (ring gauge) of cigars, the girth of the shank has no effect on the quality of the smoking experience. The shank can be straight or curved (bent) to the extent of one-eighth, one-quarter, one-half, three-quarters, or full.

The portion of the end of the shank that joins with the stem does so in a mortise-and-tenon joint.

THE STEM

The length of a pipe is determined by its stem. These are the common lengths and shapes:

Churchwarden: Round, long and narrow, tapered.

Cutty: Stubby and round. (Because it brings the bowl of the pipe close to the face it's also known as a "nose-warmer.")

Dudeen: Round, medium to long.

Flush: Round, medium.

Saddle: Diamond-shaped and then tapered, medium.

THE MOUTHPIECE

Connected by a tenon to the mortise of the shank, this tapering extension between shank and lips is also called a bit.

There are three types of bit opening, known as the lip:

Orific: A round hole.

Steck: A hole at the top of the bit.

Wedge: Flat and wide.

Most mouthpieces are made of vulcanite (hard rubber). Others may be of ivory, horn, bone, plastic, or amber, a resin that has become fossilized. As those who saw the movie *Jurassic Park* know, some ambers may hold trapped creatures from which, in theory, DNA can be extracted so as to clone and reproduce ancient life (such as dinosaurs, although ambers usually contain an insect). Amber is found mainly along the Baltic coast of Prussia, as well as in Sicily. Colors range from dull and greenish yellow to red.

PIPE SHAPES AND STYLES

Apple: Smallish, slightly flattened-looking round bowl with straight or slightly bent stem.

Billiard: Ample bowl whose height equals the length of its straight stem.

Bulldog: A rakish-looking pipe with diamond-shaped shank and stem, and a bowl that bulges widely to a carved band two-thirds of the way to the top, after which it tapers inward.

Canadian: Straight with an extra-long shank and short bit.

Dublin: Angled sides and a top that is considerably wider than the bottom.

Freehand: Irregularly sculpted and rugged-looking.

Poker: Cylindrical and straight with a flat bottom.

Pot: Short, flat top, rounded bottom.

Prince: Similar to the pot style but with a short shank and a long, slightly curving, elegant stem.

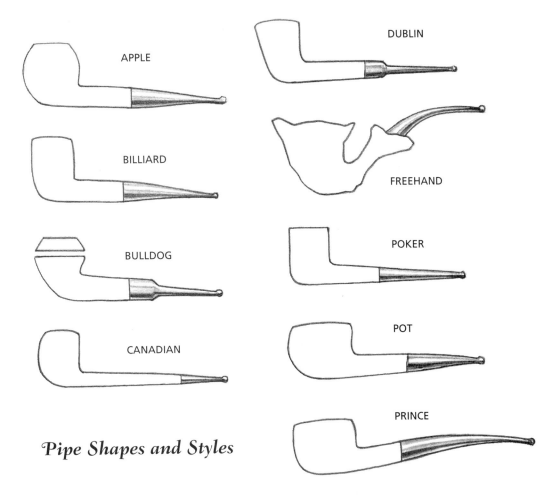

APPLE

BILLIARD

BULLDOG

CANADIAN

DUBLIN

FREEHAND

POKER

POT

PRINCE

Pipe Shapes and Styles

FILTERS

Intended to cool and refine the smoke and to control the problem of bitter fluids getting into the mouth, filters made of metal and paper may be inserted into the air channel between stem and shank. They are to pipe smokers what holders are to smokers of cigars: a matter of taste and choice. There has been a long-running and fierce debate as to their propriety. Weber's book left the decision up to the individual. Herment's dismissed filters as "gadgets" and "a useless and perverse luxury" that spoil smoking by clogging up the pipe. A few pipes have been designed to eliminate wetness in other ways. (See chapter 5.)

MAKING A BRIAR PIPE

THE BURL

The portion of the heath tree (bush) that is used in the making of pipes is the burl: the extremely hard, knobby point from which all

The Making of a Pipe . . .

Photographs © by Kevin Gordon

. . . from a block of briar to the finished product.

Two blocks of briar showing difference in graining.

The shape and size of the block and the nature of the grain dictate the shape and style of the pipe.

Making briar pipes is a one-at-a-time process. A block of briar is selected and examined.

The block is polished to accentuate its graining.

The block is hewn by sawing or sanding to create the rough shape of a pipe and shank. Except for the introduction of electricity to run a shaping wheel, the method of making pipes has changed very little since the briar pipe made its debut in Europe in the mid-nineteenth century.

A drill is used to make the bowl of a roughly shaped pipe.

Refining the shape on a sanding wheel.

The shaped pipe is polished, both bowl and shank.

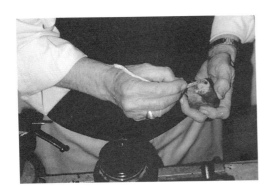

Staining the pipe brings out the rich color and character of the natural briar grain.

Wax is put on the brush of the wheel, then applied to the pipe bowl. The wax both protects the wood and enhances the darkening of the briar as it is smoked.

Finished pipe with stem attached.

the roots extend. After being dug out of the ground it is cut into rough shapes. A chunk of cut burl is called an *ébauchon* (pronounced eh-bah-SHON). After being inspected and deemed free of flaws, these very rough blocks are graded as to size, color, and grain pattern.

CURING

After being steamed or boiled to extract sap, the *ébauchons* are slow-dried in air in ventilated sheds. To prevent cracking the wood is periodically moistened. Inspected again for flaws, they are sorted by size and graded for quality. The lowest of the grades is standard (highly flawed and used in very cheap pipes). In ascending order of perfection the others are: premium (most pipes on the market are of this quality), extra, and double extra quality. The higher the quality classification, the costlier the pipe.

SHAPING

This process begins by cutting the *ébauchon* into an L-shaped block. This is placed on a lathe for honing to the desired shape. The shank is also shaped, and the airhole drilled. The stem is fitted and the shank is sandpapered to conform with the stem.

GRAIN

It is during the shaping process that the grain of the briar becomes most evident. There are four varieties:

Straight: Parallel vertical graining.

Flame: Curved and swirled graining that appears to be in the shape of a flame.

Burl: Curved and swirled pattern.

Cross-cut: A mixture.

FINISHING

As in all woodworking, when the pipe's shaping has been completed, its surface is smoothed through fine sandpapering, then buffed. At this point it is ready to be colored by staining (to enhance the appearance of the grain). This step is followed by application of a coating of wax, both to magnify the beauty of the wood and to protect it.

There are three basic finishes:

Smooth: Sleek and highly polished.

Sandblasted: A rugged surface, also known as a rustic, shell, or thorn finish; it's lighter in weight because it has less wood. This technique is often used to eliminate flaws.

Carved: Freehand or decoratively sculpted (sometimes to disguise flaws).

Briars of the highest quality (that is, free of flaws) are called "firsts" and bring the highest prices at retail sale. But "seconds" prove to be very fine pipes.

Unquestionably the most widely smoked pipe in the world, the briar has inspired numerous poets to extoll its virtues, including the anonymous nineteenth-century author who sat at dusk beneath "the old beechen tree" with brilliant October leaves and penned:

> *O my briarwood pipe!*
> *What a medley of forms you create;*
> *Every puff of white smoke seems a vision as fair*
> *As the poet's bright dream, and like dreams fades in air,*
> *While the dreamer dreams of his fate.*

Cherrywood

As noted earlier, this pipe is made from the wood of the wild cherry tree with the bark left on. Consequently, it is not shaped on a lathe, but left with its natural surface. The lathe is used only to hollow out the bowl, and to drill a hole to fit the stem. This is made from a twig of the same tree and fitted with an ebonite mouthpiece. The taste is on the strong side and slightly aromatic. This wood's chief defect is that it chars easily.

Rosewood

Known in French as *palissandre,* the Brazilian rosetree is a medium-hard wood with a rich aroma and colors ranging from purple-brown to burnt sienna. Made in the West Indies in a manner similar to the briar, rosewood pipes are small and delicate and tend to smoke hot. They usually do not come with a mouthpiece, but one may be attached with a metal band.

Other Woods

Among other trees and shrubs employed in the making of pipes are Italian olive; African ebony; American birch, hickory, maple, and red gum; switch sorrel; wild lilac; and manzanita.

Meerschaum

Of the nonwood pipes, none is so prized and praised as the one that had its beginning deep in the earth around Eskişehir, Turkey. It was a lightweight, porous white mineral that, as noted earlier, the Germans called meerschaum (sea surf), and that proved ideal for shaping and exquisitely detailed carving.

The generally accepted account of the making of the first meerschaum pipe sets the date sometime in 1723. When a chunk of the unusual mineral was presented to Count Andrassy of Austria, the dedicated pipe smoker immediately recognized its potential and handed it over to his cobbler, Karl Kowates (in some versions the name is Kovacs), who enjoyed a reputation as an expert woodcarver. The result was a pair of pipes—one for the count and the other for Kowates.

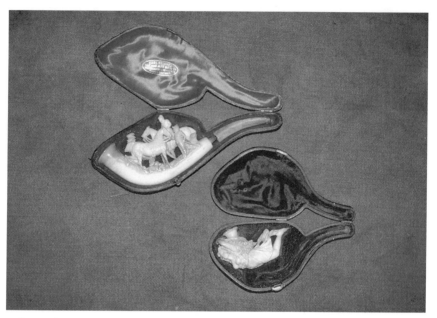

Soft meerschaum proved an exquisite medium for elaborate carvings. © Kevin Gordon

The shoemaker immediately made a fascinating discovery about the nature of meerschaum. After his first smoke, he noticed that wherever his wax-stained fingers had touched the bowl, the white had turned golden brown. Deducing that the wax had been the cause of the change in hue, and wanting his unusual pipe to have a uniform appearance, he waxed the whole bowl, lit it up again, and found that the entire surface had darkened slightly.

As Kowates, Count Andrassy, and generations of meerschaum smokers have learned, the more the pipe is smoked, the deeper and mellower becomes the tone of its meerschaum. The process was noted by a French pipe expert, E. Clerc, in 1866. He wrote, "These hues progress from a golden white to a rich brown, passing through the delicate pink of a china rose, a faint yellow, a golden yellow, pale orange, pinky brown, a light leather brown, warm brown, red brown, dark brown to an eventual black."

MAKING MEERSCHAUMS

In the decidedly unpoetic language of chemistry, meerschaum is a mixture of hydrogen, magnesium, silica, and oxygen. To the geologist it is sedimentary rock of metamorphosed strata that includes aeons-old seashells. As such, it must be mined. If it is in deposits near the surface, picks and shovels suffice. But most of the material lies deeper, requiring the digging of pits or, as in coal and gold mining, the sinking of shafts and tunnels.

Brought to the surface, it is dirty white in color and in crude chunks of varying sizes that must be cleaned of sand, dirt, and other debris. To purify the color the magnesite is boiled in milk. To make the soft, spongelike material more malleable it is kneaded with wax and linseed oil. Like brier burls, the substance must be rough-cut into pipe-shaped blocks.

Refining and shaping of the bowls is done either on lathes or with sculpting tools in the hands of artisans. Throughout the shaping process the meerschaum must be kept moist. When the desired configuration is attained the pipe maker rubs and polishes it, and treats it with a wax that serves to neutralize elements in the meerschaum that the heat of burning tobacco would quickly carbonize. Honed further with pumice powder or mutton bone, the bowl is glazed with lime and tallow, given a final buffing, and soaked in boiling beeswax. (It is this step that imbues the meerschaum with its ability to change color as it is smoked.) When cooled and dried the pipe gets its last polishing before being fitted with either a push-in or a screw-on bit, usually of molded plastic.

Being porous, a meerschaum need not be positioned in a rack with the bowl down for drainage of moisture.

Because of the fragility of meerschaum pipes and to maintain their beauty, they are generally sold in fitted cases. This feature has always made them very attractive as gifts. Evidence of just how welcome the presentation of a meerschaum can be is found in "On the Gift of a Meerschaum Pipe," a six-stanza poem dedicated to a friend by James Russell Lowell. It began:

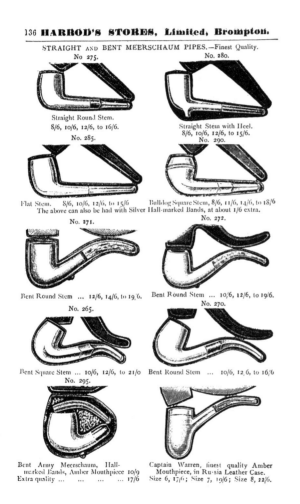

136 **HARROD'S STORES, Limited, Brompton.**

STRAIGHT AND BENT MEERSCHAUM PIPES.—Finest Quality.

No 275.

Straight Round Stem.
8/6, 10/6, 12/6, to 16/6.

No. 280.

Straight Stem with Heel.
8/6, 10/6, 12/6, to 15/6.

No. 285.

Flat Stem.   8/6, 10/6, 12/6, to 15/6
The above can also be had with Silver Hall-marked Bands, at about 1/6 extra.

No. 290.

Bulldog Square Stem, 8/6, 11/6, 14/6, to 18/6

No. 271.

Bent Round Stem ... 12/6, 14/6, to 19/6.

No. 272.

Bent Round Stem ... 10/6, 12/6, to 19/6.

No. 265.

Bent Square Stem ... 10/6, 12/6, to 21/0

No. 270.

Bent Round Stem ... 10/6, 12/6, to 16/6

No. 295.

Bent Army Meerschaum, Hall-marked Bands, Amber Mouthpiece 10/9
Extra quality 17/6

Captain Warren, finest quality Amber Mouthpiece, in Russia Leather Case.
Size 6, 17/6; Size 7, 19/6; Size 8, 22/6.

Nineteenth-century Harrod's catalog page showing the London store's selection of meerschaum pipes.
New York Public Library

The pipe came safe, and
welcome, too,
As anything must from
you;
A meerschaum pure,
'twould float as light . . .
Mixture divine of foam
and clay,
From both it stole the
best away. . . .

Numerous meerschaum lovers who fancied themselves poets also took up pens with praise, such as this unsigned paean:

Let revellers sing of their wine,
As they toss it in ecstasy down,
But the bowl I call for is thine,
With its deepening amber and brown,
My Meerschaum!

And there was "The Dreamer's Pipe," published more than a century ago in the pages of the *New Orleans Times Democrat*:

Meerschaum thing with amber tip,
Clutched between the dreamer's lip,
Fragrant odors from thy bowl
Mingling with the dreamer's soul;
Curling wreaths of smoke ascending,
Comfort sweet with incense blending.
Joy and peace and solace sending
To the dreamer's heart.

While this meerschaum of such exultant and dreamy poetry is also used to line bowls of pipes made of other substances, it has proved to be a perfect fit for another featherweight pipe that is made from a South African gourd.

The Calabash

For decades on radio and television the bulbous-nosed comedian Jimmy "The Schnozz" Durante sported an old beat-up fedora and a gravelly voice, and puzzled his audiences by ending his show with, "Good night, Mrs. Calabash, wherever you are." This left mystified listeners wondering if the salutation was just another Durante gag, or a code of some kind that only Mrs. Calabash would appreciate. If a real person, might she be, perhaps, a former girlfriend? A schoolteacher from Durante's youth? A racehorse? Or could it be possible that there existed somewhere a woman who'd had the dubious fate to go through life married to somebody named after a cumbersome and ungainly pipe?

MAKING A CALABASH

Whereas meerschaums and briars are given their shapes after being removed from the ground, the calabash is formed by controlling the growth of the gourd to result in a hooked neck. Harvested, it is trimmed at both ends and then hollowed. Left to dry, it's given a polishing and waxing. A meerschaum bowl is then inserted, followed by attachment of a plastic or hard-rubber bit.

Its long curving stem, the meerschaum lining of the bowl, and the placement of the airhole at the bottom of the bowl make the calabash a very cool and dry smoking experience. It is also a very efficient furnace that allows the tobacco to burn completely.

Of the almost infinite variety of pipes made to fit into the hand the calabash is the least likely to be toted about in a coat pocket. Although so light as to be virtually weightless, its bulk dictates sedentary smoking, perhaps on a brisk evening with a pile of crackling logs in the fireplace, a glass of brandy within easy reach, and an absorbing book in hand, preferably a mystery.

If the choice of reading matter should be a Sherlock Holmes story, do not expect to find the resident sleuth of 221B Baker Street puffing away on a calabash. Nowhere in the prose of Sir Arthur Conan Doyle will you find any mention of one. The big yellow-gold pipe with the long, gracefully arched stem was put in Holmes's hand not by the author of the fifty-six stories and four novels, but by motion picture comedians (see chapter 9).

BRIAR CALABASHES

Shaped like a gourd calabash, these S-shaped Dublin-style pipes are half to full bent with a protruding lip around the rim of the bowl. Holmes probably smoked one. But if Dr. Watson did not observe Holmes smoking a briar as he pondered the intricacies of a fresh case, he was likely to observe "thrusting out like the bill of some strange bird" the longish stem of "his black clay pipe."

Clay

Little has changed in the making of this granddaddy of pipes since it was first produced in England a few years before Sir Walter Raleigh's explorers stumbled upon tobacco in Virginia. The basic method then and now involves forming the clay in a two-part mold made of metal, then baking it in kilns.

Before the clay is ready for firing, however, it must go through a laborious process of preparation that in some ways is akin to making

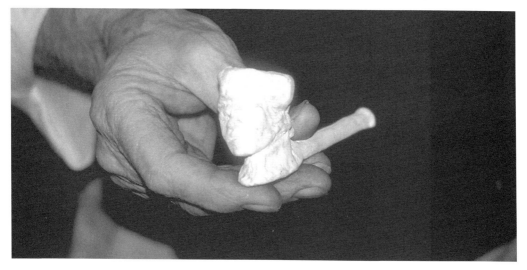

A portrait of Paul Revere forms the bowl of a clay pipe made by Robert Peretti in celebration of the U.S. Bicentennial in 1976. © Kevin Gordon

bread. After soaking in water the doughlike clay is rolled by hand into long, thin tubes and left to set.

When the material is judged ready a wire is inserted to form the airhole. With the wire remaining in place the clay tube is pressed into the mold to form the shape of the bowl. Some molds are engraved with decorative designs, emblems, or the insignias of the maker, which are then embossed into the soft clay.

Following partial drying, the mold and the hole-making wire are removed. The pipe is examined, its excess clay trimmed, and it is placed along with numerous others in the kiln.

After firing, colored varnish or plain lacquer is applied as a sealant. The pipes are not fitted with bits.

As to the taste of a clay pipe, Georges Herment wrote that it is "slightly rough, and is accompanied by the healthy and fortifying smell of moist clay—a primitive enjoyment, secret, yielding itself with a truly miserly parsimony. It is the elusive smell of Nature when a sudden downpour of rain or a high wind has swept things clean."

But clays do break easily, perhaps to leave the dedicated clay smoker feeling as desolate as the unknown soul who long ago mused on the destiny of things made of clay, whether a pipe or a human being:

> *Neglected now it lies, a cold clay form,*
> *So late with living inspirations warm;*
> *Type of all other creatures formed of clay—*
> *What more than it for an epitaph have they?*

Corncob

A persuasive argument may be made that the United States of America could not have come into existence, or survived and prospered, were it not for corn (whether as the abundant foodstuff of a hungry world or as whiskey for its imbibers) and tobacco.

It was probably inevitable—it certainly was fitting—that the two were brought together as the only variety of pipe that in the modern world can be truly called American.

Over a century ago in "The Pipe You Make Yourself" a poet named Henry E. Brown wrote:

> *Jest take a common corn cob and whittle out the middle,*
> *Then plug up one end of it as tight as any fiddle;*
> *Fit a stem into th' side an' lay her on th' shelf,*
> *An' when she's dry you take her down, that pipe you*
>   *made yourself.*

The formula works today. But because this is America, the desire for a corncob pipe, as in the case of almost everything else, can be satisfied by simply buying one.

The Missouri Meerschaum Company's letterhead, which depicts its factory in Washington, Missouri.

What has changed since Henry Brown waxed poetic is that today there are eighteen styles of corncob pipe being made by one dominant manufacturer. Since Henry Tibbe sold out his first examples of the pipe in 1869, his Missouri Meerschaum Company has made his hometown—Washington, Missouri—as a company brochure boasts, "the Corn Cob Capital of the World."

MAKING CORNCOB PIPES

Tibbe's initial pipes were made of cobs from ordinary corn (open-pollinated). Today's are manufactured from a special white hybrid corn developed by the University of Missouri. The variety is grown by farmers in the Washington area from seeds (provided by the firm) that produce big, thick, tough cobs.

In a case of "new is not necessarily better," modern machinery designed to shell the corn turned out to be disastrous. It broke the cobs and made them unusable. Consequently, shelling is still being done by machinery dating to the 1930s.

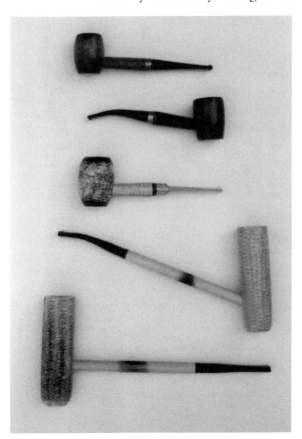

Mechanization notwithstanding, corncob-pipe making requires a lot of hands-on operations.

Production begins with the cobs being dumped into a chute that sends them to the lowest level of the three-story factory. With remaining husks removed, the cobs are fed into saws and cut into uniform lengths. These are tumbled onto a conveyor belt for grading and sorting by size. Holes are then bored, and the cobs moved to four turning machines for shaping. (Some larger pipes are turned by hand.)

There are eighteen different styles of corncob pipe produced by the Missouri Meerschaum Company today. Pictured are different pipe styles featuring a variety of bowl shapes and stems.
Missouri Meerschaum Company

These rough pipes are now ready for application of Henry Tibbe's invention—the white plaster sealing coat that solved the problem of wetness. Dried and sanded, the pipes are ready for the final stages of production: the boring of the stem hole and application of varnish.

The wood stem is glued in the bowl and a ring and plastic bit are added, along with a Missouri Meerschaum label on the flat bottom of the pipe.

Notable corncob pipe smokers include the comic-strip characters Mammy Yokum in "L'il Abner" and squinty-eyed, spinanch-eating Popeye; and the literary world's Mark Twain and Robert Frost.

The Picta 1 *is one of sixteen pipes in Ser Jacapo's* Picta Collection *which pays homage to the pipes represented in van Gogh's paintings. This particular pipe was inspired by the one portrayed in van Gogh's self-portrait, shown on page 58.* Ser Jacapo della Gemma, Italy

The Domina 1998, *a limited edition in Ser Jacapo's "Pipe of the Year" series. Highly prized and collectible, only 333 pipes are crafted in this series each year.* Ser Jacapo della Gemma, Italy

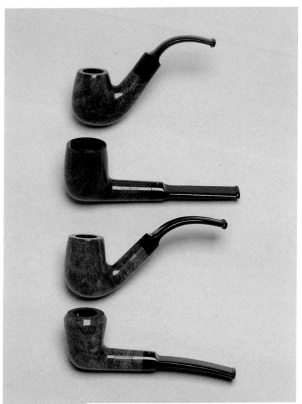

The Londoner, Garnet, Guinea *and* Sovereign, *four distinct pipe shapes and finishes offered among many others by Barling of England.* James Norman, Ltd.

The Barling family's tradition as English silversmiths can be seen in the fine silver mountings on these late-nineteenth-century Barling pipes. James Norman, Ltd.

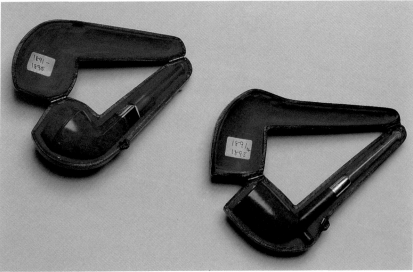

Each Caminetto pipe is handmade and fitted with a "metacrillato" stem which never tarnishes. James Norman, Ltd.

The Bent, Billiard, Bulldog, *and* Dublin *(shown l. to r.) are reproductions of some of Peterson's most popular pipes first crafted in the early 1900's. Each pipe is silver mounted and hallmarked.* Peterson of Dublin

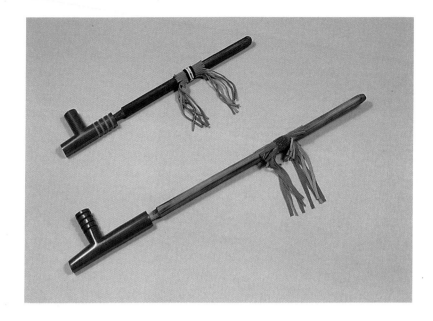

Authentic calumet "peace" pipes. Pipestone Indian Shrine Association

The futuristic design of the Cybele by venerable French pipe maker, Butz-Choquin, debuted in 1996 to commemorate the thirtieth anniversary of the Confrérie des Maîtres Pipiers de Saint-Claude. *The briar is combined with a marquetry of sycamore, lemon tree, Zebrano, and amourette, among other exotic woods; the pipes are shown fitted with lucite mouthpieces.* Société des pipes Butz-Choquin.

Pipes from Butz-Choquin's 1998 Jubile collection. This style became famous in the nineteenth-century as a sign of resistance in German-occupied Lorraine between 1870 and 1918. If you entered a bar smoking this pipe, you thereby declared your support for France. Société des pipes Butz-Choquin.

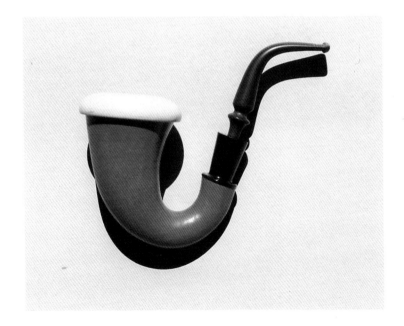

Made from a specially-grown South African gourd, the bulky but graceful calabash, with its long, curved shank and stem and meerschaum-lined bowl, provides a cool, dry smoke. So light as to be almonst weightless, the calabash invites an evening spent by a fireplace, a glass of brandy at hand and an absorbing book to read—preferably a mystery. Kevin Gordon

Three examples of the more than eighty basic shapes and models of Savinelli pipes. The company was founded by Achille Savinelli in Milan in 1876.
Savinelli Inc., USA

This Ladies Companion Set was featured in an Alfred Dunhill catalog dated 1921. The ladies pipe features interchangeable mouthpieces—one short, one long—and four bowls cut from one piece of briarwood: two are suitable for tobacco, one for ladies-size cigars, and one for cigarettes. Alfred Dunhill Pipes Limited, London

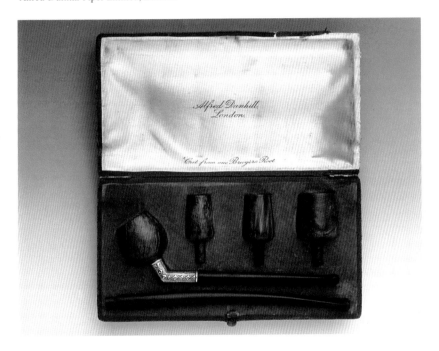

This Prince of Wales "Profile Pipe" was specially commissioned by Alfred Dunhill for Edward, Prince of Wales—later Edward VIII, then Duke of Windsor. The bowl of the Bruyère pipe was hand carved so as to feature a profile of his face. Alfred Dunhill Pipes Limited, London

The Ashton Sovereign pipe. Company founder William Ashton-Taylor, who began his pipe-making career as a fifteen-year-old Dunhill apprentice, travels to Italy twice yearly to select for himself the very finest briar wood for his pipes. Ashton Distributors, photograph by Callaghan Photography

5

A Sweet Smoke

There may be comrades in this world,
*   As stanch and true as steel.*
There are: and by their friendships firm
*   Is life made only real.*
But, after all, of all these hearts
*   That close to mine entwine,*
None lie so near, nor seem so dear
*   As this old pipe of mine.*

—ELTON J. BUCKLEY

Go into any store that purveys pipes and at least one wall will feature a display of hundreds of enticing choices that will make you want to cry out, "So many pipes to smoke and so little time in life to do so!"

This was not always so in the United States. While the pipe had flourished in the colonies and after independence, in the era following the Civil War it was the cigar that was to capture the smoker's dollar and continue to claim it right through World War I, only to be eclipsed in the 1920s and thereafter by the cigarette. Throughout this long period the briar pipe had been an imported product that carried a high price. Not until the 1930s did pipe smoking begin to make a kind of comeback, sparked by the availability of lower-cost, machine-made pipes that were mass-marketed by domestic firms. Because smoking these proved less costly in the long run than cigarettes, brands such as

"So many pipes to smoke and so little time in life to do so."
© Kevin Gordon

Kaywoodie, Medico, and Yello-Bole flourished. (These American-made pipes are examined in more detail later in this chapter.)

Today, to look through brochures of pipe manufacturers or store catalogs is to be dazzled by a bewildering array of sizes, shapes, and styles. A recent pocket-size leaflet for Peterson, for example, depicted sixty "Classical and Unusual" shapes. Known as the "Old English Collection" and re-created from designs of the 1930s and 1940s, they were offered singly or in a presentation box of twelve. Special Peterson pipes also included models to mark various anniversaries, including the centennial of the company (1975); a Mark Twain commemorative; the Millennium, marking the one-thousandth anniversary of the founding of Dublin, Ireland; and a set of seven known as the Sherlock Holmes Classic Collection, whose members were each named for a Sherlockian character, place, or object. The first to be issued was in honor of Holmes, of course, and it was followed by the Baskerville, Baker Street, Deerstalker, Squire, Professor (Moriarty), and Dr. Watson. A follow-up series, "The Return of Sherlock Holmes," honored Holmes's landlady, Mrs. Hudson; his brother, Mycroft; Inspector Lestrade; the infamous blackmailer Charles Augustus Milverton; and Basil Rathbone, whose movie-Holmes always smoked a Peterson. (More about this company's unique pipes will also be found later in this chapter.)

Maker's Marks

Since the earliest makers of clay pipes in England introduced markings on stems and bowls to identify themselves or their customers, pipe manufacturers have found many ways to hallmark their wares.

Peterson pipes are identified by silver bands between shank and stem and an elegantly scrolled P.

A sampling of clay pipe maker's marks.

Sasieni of London's symbol is a triangle consisting of four white dots that signify its line of "4-Dot Classics."

A single dot on a stem is the symbol of Alfred Dunhill. One of Britain's oldest and most esteemed makers of elegant pipes, the company's list of styles seems endless.

Many others imprint a set of initials or a unique pattern. And there are innumerable pipes that bear names of tobacconists' shops. These are often "seconds" from major manufacturers that the dealers have named after themselves. For the buyer on an austerity budget these can be both economical and excellent smokes. Don't shun a pipe just because it's a "second."

How to Decide?

In *The Pleasures of Pipe Smoking* Carl Weber wrote, "To the serious pipe smoker, buying a pipe may represent an adventure only slightly less terrifying and final than selecting one's cemetery plot."

Others have likened the act to buying a car or house, or even proposing marriage.

Ludicrous comparisons, of course. Before you kick the bucket you can always pick another place to be planted. A car that turns out to be a lemon, or simply tiresome, can be traded in for another. A house may be renovated or sold. And half of all marriages end in divorce. But once you have smoked a pipe only to discover you've blundered in buying it, there's no taking it back.

While some used pipes may turn up for sale in estate auctions and flea markets, and some may be deemed worthy of being recycled as collectibles (see chapter 10), a used pipe is like someone else's old pair of shoes—interesting, perhaps, and even quaint, but recommended only to those willing to do all that may be needed to make them serviceable again. (For the art of reviving old pipes, also see chapter 10.)

A used pipe may also be treasured by the sentimental. In one of the Basil Rathbone Sherlock Holmes movies, for instance, Inspector Lestrade—in the mistaken belief that Holmes had been killed—sneakily pocketed one of Sherlock's well-charred briars as a memento, only to find the not-dead-after-all detective searching for it. Touched by Lestrade's gesture of respect, Holmes let him keep it. Considering the strong shag that Sherlock preferred, and given his habit of packing it with the dottles of the previous day's smoking, one can only hope that before the Scotland Yarder lit it up he took the precaution of cleaning and sweetening it.

Factors considered by Weber to be essential in buying a new pipe were: price, function, what it is made of, the shape of bowl and stem, and *the shape of the buyer's face.*

"Portly men with round faces look better with curved pipes," he wrote, while long stems favor slender faces, notwithstanding the fact that the lean (even gaunt) sleuth of 221B Baker Street favored curved stems.

In *The Ultimate Pipe Book* Richard Carleton Hacker began his chapter on picking the right pipe by also citing how a pipe looks in someone's mouth. Of three elements to be taken into account when buying a pipe he wrote: "It has to fit your character, it has to look good, and it has to make *you* look good."

The pipe should also *feel* good. When considering one, hold it to test its feel in your hand. Judge the texture of the bowl's finish. Then visualize it as part of your silhouette.

But the crucial factor in selecting a pipe, as in everything in life, is price. Remember that you get what you pay for.

Filling and Lighting

1. Load tobacco a little at a time, packing it neither too loosely nor too tightly.

2. Apply flame evenly to the surface of the tobacco.

Bright and shiny, a new briar is a beautiful object, but, as a nineteenth-century writer on the subject of pipes, John Baine, warned, "It is like a new baby and must be treated tenderly."

Breaking In

Your new briar pipe is not a baby, but neither is it like a new car. The bowl is not a gas tank. It's made of wood, not of metal. Do not immediately "fill 'er up" and go speeding off.

The object is to build up the caking of the interior of the bowl *gradually.* Proper caking ensures a cooler smoke.

Some experts recommend that before you put in any tobacco you coat the inside of the bowl with a thin layer of honey. This aids in the caking process. But correct caking is also attainable by proper packing, which means little by little, about a fifth of a bowl at a time: one-fifth for the first smoke, two-fifths for the second, and so on until you've reached the top. Smoke each stage to the bottom of the bowl.

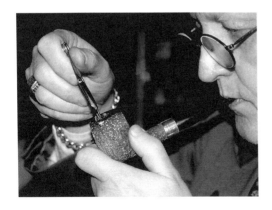

3. Gently tamp the lighted tobacco while drawing smoke; relight if necessary.

4. Puff slowly and easily.

Photo series © Kevin Gordon

Filling the Bowl

First, be sure the pipe is emptied of the ash and tobacco left over from a previous smoke, and that it is cooled and rested. Second, check the air passages of shank and stem for blockages.

Once the pipe has been broken in and is ready for day-to-day use, the tobacco may be loaded to the top of the bowl. In doing this, don't pack too tightly. You can test the air flow by drawing on the stem. You will know right away if it is too tight, because you won't be able to get air through. Remove the tobacco and start over. Each successive addition of tobacco should have a springy feel. Smooth the surface with a gentle tamping.

Lighting

Here's an aspect of smoking pipes that is rife with heated disagreement. Should the flame be that produced by a mechanical lighter or with a match, and if a match, a wooden one or paper?

Proponents of wooden matches point out that because they are larger than the paper kind, they burn longer. This is true, but paper matches are generally available for free from tobacconists, while wooden matches usually must be bought, and they are not inexpensive. Some restaurants of the classier variety may provide patrons with pocket-size boxes of wooden matches, but because of the inroads made by antismoking zealots, this little amenity is becoming an increasingly endangered species.

The flames of both wooden and paper matches should be allowed to burn a bit before being applied to the tobacco. This removes sulfur or other elements that could taint the tobacco's taste.

Disdainers of lighters fear the infusion of the tobacco with the taste of the igniting chemical or gas. They also claim that a lighter's flame is more likely to scorch the bowl rim. However, lighter enthusiasts point out that not only are they convenient but they also don't go out, as matches frequently do, during the process of lighting. This is often the result of the smoker blowing out the match as he puffs. Whichever means of lighting you employ, apply the flame to the tobacco evenly as you draw air through it in order to produce even burning.

Then lightly pat the tobacco with a tamping tool. This lessens the chance of the tobacco going out. Should you have a high tolerance for pain you can also tamp it with your fingertip. (More on tampers and other gadgetry may be found in chapter 7.)

Proper Smoking

Slow and easy does it. A pipe is not a cigarette and you are not Humphrey Bogart in a movie flashback as you wait in the rain on a Parisian train platform, puffing anxiously amid Nazi-fleeing Frenchmen while the ever-loyal piano-playing Dooley Wilson thinks you have gone nuts as you search with increasing puzzlement and frustration for Ingrid Bergman in the hope that she'll show up in time to rush into your open arms to go with you to a safer place, perhaps in North Africa (Casablanca, for instance), where, if the situation gets worse, you can catch a flight to Lisbon and then the Pan Am Clipper to America. But if you happen to be wanted by the police in the United States, you'll always have Paris.

This scene would never have played if Rick Blaine had been a pipe smoker. As has been shown scientifically, pipe smokers do not rush into anything (Sherlock Holmes excepted).

"The pipe should provide enjoyment, not frustration," was the sage advice of Richard Carleton Hacker in *The Ultimate Pipe Book.* "After all, pipe smoking is among the gentlest and most relaxing of all human activities, and these are the legacies to which every pipe smoker falls heir, whether he smokes an inexpensive corncob or a priceless freehand straight grain."

A poet whose name went unrecorded wrote:

> *Sweet smoking pipe; bright glowing stove,*
>   *Companion still of my retreat,*
> *Thou dost my gloomy thoughts remove,*
>   *And purge my brain with gentle heat.*

SMOKING COOL

While fire in a pipe bowl is elementary, the heat produced can be a problem. Smoke too fast and even the finest briar pipe can get too hot to handle. This also happens if you smoke hard, so don't.

Neither is smoking in a strong draft or high winds a good idea. You might appear dashing while smoking a pipe in a speeding convertible with the top down, but you won't enjoy it. And you run the grave risk of you and the auto's interior being showered with red-hot embers. There is little so disheartening as burned upholstery and clothing with tiny holes in it. You can also wind up with searing ash in your eyes.

Too much heat can also result in too much charring and spoil the pipe, a condition known as "burnout."

If you find a pipe getting too hot, set it aside and let it cool for a time, then relight and try again. Excessive heat may also be avoided by not messing around with the ash as it accumulates atop the burning tobacco. Don't shake it out. Leaving it in place affords a cooler smoke.

Finally, as you tamp the burning tobacco during your smoke, do not press hard; just press sufficiently to keep the burning process going.

KEEPING A PIPE LIT

Rare is the pipe smoker who needs only one match to start a pipe and rarer still is he who does not have to relight. The phenomenon of pipes going out in midsmoke is so common that contests are held to see who uses the fewest matches to keep a pipe lit. However, a relit pipe is not like a cigar that has gone out and been started again. Such a stogie will taste stronger, even bitter, while restarted pipe tobacco exhibits no change in its flavor. Therefore, you need not worry about interrupting your smoking.

But do be careful about sticking a warm pipe in a pocket. This author ruined two sports jackets that way. If your pipe is set aside until smoking may be resumed, the best place to put it is in an ashtray or rack. Whenever you finish it, though, there are steps to be taken to be sure it's properly prepared for your next smoke.

Emptying a Pipe

The perfectly smoked pipe will have at the bottom of its bowl only a small amount of ash. But perfection is elusive. Most of the time the bottom will contain a not-very-pleasant-looking or -smelling wet gob of gunk with a name that's more amusing than it is—dottle.

The understandable impulse is to turn the pipe upside down and rap it hard on something to dislodge the dottle and knock it out. Don't, or if you can't resist the impulse, simply tap the bowl in the palm of your hand. This avoids damaging the pipe. A better way is to use the small spoonlike tool made just for the purpose of scooping out dottle. Material may also stick to the interior sides of the bowl. Use a scraping tool to dislodge it. With the bowl cleaned, run a pipe cleaner through stem and shank. (These and various implements for cleaning and caring for pipes are discussed and described in chapter 7.)

Long-Term Care

The following advice represents the accumulated wisdom of pipe makers, tobacconists, authors, and other experts on lifetime maintenance:

1. Use a pipe cleaner after every smoke.

2. Wipe and buff the exterior of the pipe after each use.

3. Store in a well-ventilated spot out of direct sunlight, which can accelerate oxidation, causing fading of the pipe's natural color.

4. Use a pipe rack to keep pipes upright, allowing drainage.

5. Clean the bowl periodically, leaving a light caking.

6. Every six months treat the mouthpiece, stem, and shank with a pipe sweetener; keep the bit free of dirt and grime.

Sweetening a Pipe

Sad to say, with much use and passage of time even the best briar pipe can exude an unpleasant smell. Getting rid of this odor is known as "sweetening." It's achieved by applying a cleaning solvent made especially for sweetening and used with a pipe cleaner. This liquid is sold in all pipe stores. Smokers, such as this author, who also enjoy spiritous drinks have been known to sweeten pipes by dipping a pipe cleaner into their favorite libation. Sweetening is commonly carried out semiannually.

This process and the others named above for caring for briar pipes may also be used in tending to corncob pipes and delicate meerschaums. However, bare-handed manipulation of meerschaum bowls should be avoided in order to prevent skin oils and sweat from leaving blemishes and discoloration.

Treatment of clay pipes in the above manner is not recommended. You'll end up with a cracked or broken pipe. Smoke a clay until it can't be smoked further, then discard it.

Advice on the treatment and care of pipes is available from your tobacconist, and is often provided with the pipe by the manufacturer as well. A reliable guide to the quality of a pipe is the name of this manufacturer, or of the brand.

Notable Briar-Pipe Makers
(listed alphabetically)

Armellini: Made in the Cuciago region of Italy; medium-priced; machine and hand-made; marketed in the United States by the Tinder Box store chain. Good value for the price.

Ashton: Maker of the highly-prized "magnum" pipe, among others.

Ascorti: Introduced to the United States in 1980; made by Peppino Ascorti, once with the now defunct Caminetto firm (below); also sold through Tinder Box; lightweight and cool-smoking.

BBB Pipes: Britain's Best Briar is England's oldest registered pipe-making company (1847). Available as private labels and manufactured in the United States.

Baldo Baldi: Italian-made; pricey, for connoisseurs or collectors.

Barling: First produced by the Barling family, silversmiths in the 1700s, the brand was taken over by another firm in 1960 and went through several reorganizations. Manufactured on the Isle of Man in more than thirty varieties.

Butz-Choquin: Made by one of the biggest manufacturers in the Saint-Claude region of France; high-quality pipe. (It's pronounced boots-sho-CAN.)

Brebbia: Introduced in 1947 by Enea Buzzi and his cousin Achille Savinelli with the intention (in the words of Luciano Buzzi in a letter to *The Pipe Smoker's Ephemeris*) of making "high quality pipes," the firm today is a small but well-established company with a fine reputation.

Caminetto: The pipes are collectible and accordingly priced. Among the finest briars ever made.

Castello: The firm is one of the stars of Italian pipe making; its hallmark is a tiny diamond imprint on the left of the stem. Limited production keeps the price up.

Cesare: Italian-made, classically shaped, heavy.

Chapuis-Comoy: Brand name: Chacom. One of France's stellar pipe makers of the Saint-Claude region. The firm was started by a former employee of Comoy's (below) when that London-based maker closed its French factory.

Charatan: Founded in London in 1863 by Russian émigré Frederick Charatan, the firm was originally located near the Tower of London. Destroyed during the Nazi air raids of the 1940 blitz, the family operation, including its Ben Wade brand (see page 102), became part of Dunhill (below).

Comoy's: Oldest continuous briar-pipe maker in the world. Founded in France by François Comoy in 1825 to make clays, the firm began turning out briars in 1848 and moved to London in 1879. Its medium- to high-grade pipes are held in great esteem by collectors.

Dunhill: Started by Alfred Dunhill in 1907, this London-based firm is synonymous with excellence in all aspects of the tobacco trade. Its

prized pipes bear a white spot. Briars used in pipe making are classified premium grade AA. Only "firsts" get the spot.

Wally Frank, Ltd.: A familiar name in New York City for decades but,
alas, no longer in business. If you find any, the pipes are very collectible.

GBD: The initials are those of French founders (Geneval, Bondier, and
Donninger). Initally meerschaum makers, they opened operations
in London in the early 1900s to make briars. The trademark *GBD*
is surrounded by an oval.

Kaywoodie: One of the best-known brands in America, this low-cost
pipe's success not only in mass-production but also in mass-
marketing is discussed below.

Jobey: American-made. The company was once owned by Carl Weber.

W. O. Larsen: Founded in 1864; Danish maker of elegant handmades.

Lorenzo Pipes: Founded in Italy in 1900 by Lorenzo Tagliabue; the
high-quality pipes were sold under the maker's first name to dis-
tinguish them from another pipe maker named Tagliabue. Also
available with private labels.

Nording: Superb Danish freehands.

Parker-Hardcastle: Moderately priced and well made, these pipes are
manufactured in a Dunhill factory in London.

Peterson: Along with the name Dunhill, this is a pipe brand recognized for quality even by nonsmokers. It and its unique design are
discussed later in this chapter.

Pipe Dan: A long-established Danish firm producing pipes from templates; they are then hand-finished.

Preben Holm: The eponymous firm makes superb high-grade freehands in Denmark.

Radice: Also a veteran of the Caminetto company, Luigi Radice set up shop in 1981, turning out fewer than six thousand pipes a year.

Ropp: The oldest French maker (founded in 1896) is best known for its cherrywoods, but it also makes fine briars and meerschaums.

Sasieni: The firm was started by Joseph Sasieni after his stint as a pipe maker for Dunhill. Hallmarked by one, four, and eight dots.

Savinelli: Family-owned business begun in 1876 and one of Italy's earliest mass-producers of collectible briar pipes.

James Upshall: Begun in 1977 with his son by Colonel Kenneth Barnes (full name: Kenneth James Upshall-Barnes), the company quickly won acceptance in America for both its hand-turned "firsts" and "seconds" (marketed under the name Tilshead).

Ben Wade: After eighty years the firm was knocked out of business by a Nazi bombing raid on Leeds, England, but the name has been carried on by Charatan. Excellent craftsmanship and superb smokability.

What's in a Name?

It was old Sir Walter Raleigh's wordy contemporary, William Shakespeare, who immortalized the above query by raising it in a play. The question was posed by a star-crossed lover who was a member of the Capulet family, a sweet girl named Juliet. It was asked of the similarly celestial-crossed impetuous young son of the family Montague, a handsome suitor named Romeo.

So what if he was one of the Montagues, who were hated by the Capulets, and she was one of the Capulet clan, who were hated by Montagues?

What if Romeo had a different last name?

"That we call a rose," Juliet said, "by any other name would smell as sweet."

But what's true for roses is not true for pipes, nor for the problem that has vexed their smokers since John Rolfe first put one in Raleigh's hand and urged him to take that historic puff. Call a pipe by any other name and you will still have to deal with the problem of wetness and the virtual certainty that some of that very unpalatable moisture is going to find its way into your mouth.

The problem stems (no pun intended) from the fact that tobacco consists of 30 to 50 percent water. When it's lit in a pipe bowl it turns to steam. As it is drawn, along with the smoke, into the bottom of the bowl and then into the shank and stem, this steam condenses into a liquid that can be sucked through shank and stem and into the mouth, carrying with it tars, nicotine, and tongue-biting acids.

While there is no record of Sir Walter getting a mouthful of this bitter gunk as he smoked, odds are that sooner or later he did. And centuries after Sir Walter lighted the candle he hoped would never go out, the answer to the question of how to prevent this nasty influx was still being sought.

The quest has resulted in three unique styles of pipes.

PETERSON: GETTING RID OF THE GURGLE

Along with Dunhill, the pipe brand most likely to be recognized is Peterson. It's identified as a quality product even by nonsmokers,

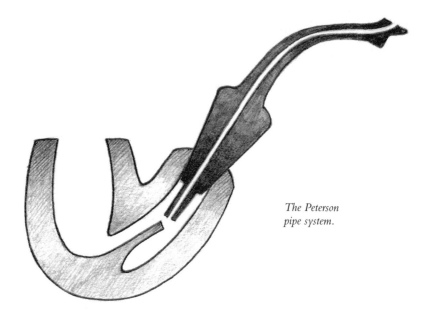

*The Peterson
pipe system.*

although they (and many veteran pipe buyers) might not be able to
explain why.

What distinguishes these Irish-made pipes is a design the company calls the "Peterson System." It handles the problem of moisture
getting into the air channel by sidetracking it.

It was the brainchild of Charles Peterson. A native of Riga, Latvia,
he invented what he called a "reservoir" in the shank to collect moisture and keep it from being drawn through the stem. The stem's design
also featured a graduated (tapered) bore. These innovations did away
with the annoying gurgling sound produced by accumulation of liquid in stem and shank and at the bottom of the bowl. Peterson's design
also allowed the same amount of smoke to go through the air channel with less puffing. And at the very end of the stem was a unique
lip: Rather than allowing smoke and heat to flow onto the tongue,

Humorist Mark Twain was an inveterate smoker of pipes and cigars. Here it's a Peterson briar in his hand, but he liked to smoke corncobs and calabashes, as well. He let it be known that if he could not smoke in Heaven, he'd head for the other place.
New York Public Library

the Peterson design put the hole on top of the lip. This directed heat to the roof of the mouth, thereby eliminating tongue bite.

After perfecting his invention Peterson patented it and, in 1890, took it to the shop of Friedrich and Heinrich Kapp. Danish pipe makers, they had been in business in Dublin, Ireland, since 1865. In short order the Kapp brothers had a partner and the firm had a new name: Kapp & Peterson.

Because the store was situated across the street from the entrance to Trinity College, its register of regular customers consisted of most of Ireland's leading literary lights, including William Butler Yeats, John Milton Synge, James Joyce, Sean O'Casey, and members of the resident company of the renowned Abbey Theatre. Ardently embracing the new-style pipe, these and other thinkers fostered the image of the intellectual as not only a pipe smoker, but a Peterson fancier. One of the pipe's American enthusiasts was Mark Twain.

Then came Basil Rathbone, who smoked a Peter-

In fourteen films with Nigel Bruce at his side as Dr. John H. Watson, Basil Rathbone's Sherlock Holmes smoked a Peterson.
New York Public Library

son pipe in all his fourteen movies as Sherlock Holmes and probably did more to enhance the status of Peterson pipes than anyone since Twain.

Unfortunately, when Rathbone made his debut as Holmes at the end of the 1930s, few Americans struggling to make ends meet in the midst of the Great Depression had the lucre to afford an expensive imported pipe of any sort, let alone a Peterson.

Four decades earlier, Vice President Thomas Marshal had said that what the country needed was a good five-cent cigar. By the end of the 1930s nickel cigars were abundant, and even they proved to be a costly indulgence. A cigar might last half an hour. No, what was needed was a way of smoking that wouldn't cost an arm and a leg; an inexpensive American-made pipe, for instance—one that would provide a clean, cool smoke.

KAYWOODIE, YELLO-BOLE, AND MEDICO FILTERED PIPES

In the middle years of the twentieth century Americans leafing through popular magazines found advertisements for a line of economical and domestically produced pipes. In addition to their low prices the pipes promised a way to deal with the persistent problem of how to contain wetness and its accompanying awful taste.

The solution, according to the maker of Kaywoodie pipes, was a built-in filter that the firm called "Drinkless." Introduced in 1931 and made of aluminum, it screwed into the bore and could cool the smoke from 850 degrees in the bowl to 82 degrees when it entered the mouth, and keep out moisture to boot. The pipe proved such an immediate success that the company moved manufacturing operations out of Union City, New Jersey, to West Broadway in New York

City, and its corporate offices into the plush surroundings of the new Rockefeller Center in the heart of Manhattan.

To meet increasing international demand for its Drinkless pipes, Kaywoodie opened an office in London in 1938 in a joint operation with Comoy's.

Originally the name of a pipe offered by the Kaufman Brothers & Bondy Company (BBB), the Kaywoodie had made its debut in 1919. It came with a hand-cut rubber mouthpiece fitted with inbore tube and push-in stem. As the business thrived, it expanded by offering a line called Yello-Bole. Introduced in 1932, the pipes did, indeed, have yellow bowls. Made of a lower-grade briar than Kaywoodies, they were produced by a BBB subsidiary, the New England Briar Pipe Company. Because one ingredient of the material used to line the bowl was honey, the Yello-Bole smoker was promised a faster and sweeter break-in of the pipe.

Another innovation was a "carburetor." This was an airhole (in another version, two holes) in the bottom of the exterior of the bowl to provide an updraft to improve combustion, take the rawness out of any tobacco and make it burn evenly, and keep the bottom of the bowl "absolutely dry."

Nor did the lip of a Yello-Bole escape modification. One version offered a "two way bit" to deliver smoke through both a hole in the end of the bit and a slot at the top. But probably the most attention-getting feature of Yello-Bole pipes was the price—one dollar—at a time when other kinds of pipes could be bought for a quarter or fifty cents.

Further expansion brought other pipe companies into the Kaywoodie organization. These included the Reiss-Premier Pipe Company and the Pacific Briar Company, a firm that experimented during World War II (when briar from Europe could not be imported) with making pipes from a burl-type wood growing on the slopes of the

Advertising for Yello-Bole and Kaywoodie pipes in the 1950s was directed at women looking for Father's Day and Christmas gifts for the men in their lives.
Kaywoodie Company

Santa Cruz Mountains of California. The substitute, called Mission Briar or manzanita, proved inadequate.

   With the end of the war, European briar again became easy to obtain at the same time that pipe smoking in America was enjoying a major comeback. This was in great part because returning GIs married the girls they had left behind and settled down in new suburban housing developments made possible by the GI Bill. As these new husbands kindled a baby boom, they also settled into the tranquil domesticity of peacetime by adopting Madison Avenue advertising

Long before public opinion surveys found that women see men who smoke pipes as "sexy," the makers of the popular Kay-woodie pipes had already made the connection.
Kaywoodie Company

agencies' picture of the ideal husband and father as content at home with wife and kids, his feet in slippers, and a pipe in his mouth. No pipe maker proved more adept at promoting this image than the Kaywoodie Company on behalf of all its products.

By the 1950s Kaywoodie pipes were selling at prices ranging from four dollars for a natural burl apple to a flame grain with amber bit for ten, and a "Centennial" billiard or a matched-grain boxed set at twenty-five. Not cheap, but the American economy was booming, and the rising tide lifted all the boats in the form of the good wages that advertisers liked to call "discretionary income," available to be spent on life's little luxuries.

A 1950s ad aimed at the Christmas gift giver also assured the buyer that pipe smoking was not harmful to the health. The ad stated that "doctors who studied the smoking habits of 187,000 men found that pipe smokers live longer than any other smokers," and that "the doctors switched to pipes themselves."

MEDICO

It was in the 1950s that Kaywoodie's success at opening new markets for pipe smoking caught the attention of another pioneer in American pipe making— S. M. Frank and Company. Founded in 1900 by Sam Frank, the company had absorbed other prominent names in the business, including William DeMuth & Company and the Manhattan Briar Pipe Company, to make one of Kaywoodie's chief rivals for the hearts of American pipe smokers— the Medico.

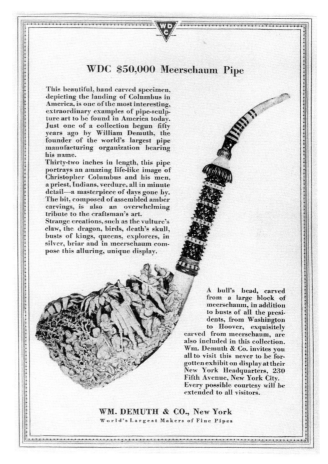

WDC $50,000 Meerschaum Pipe

This beautiful, hand carved specimen, depicting the landing of Columbus in America, is one of the most interesting, extraordinary examples of pipe-sculpture art to be found in America today. Just one of a collection begun fifty years ago by William Demuth, the founder of the world's largest pipe manufacturing organization bearing his name.

Thirty-two inches in length, this pipe portrays an amazing life-like image of Christopher Columbus and his men, a priest, Indians, verdure, all in minute detail—a masterpiece of days gone by. The bit, composed of assembled amber carvings, is also an overwhelming tribute to the craftsman's art.

Strange creations, such as the vulture's claw, the dragon, birds, death's skull, busts of kings, queens, explorers, in silver, briar and in meerschaum compose this alluring, unique display.

A bull's head, carved from a large block of meerschaum, in addition to busts of all the presidents, from Washington to Hoover, exquisitely carved from meerschaum, are also included in this collection. Wm. Demuth & Co. invites you all to visit this never to be forgotten exhibit on display at their New York Headquarters, 230 Fifth Avenue, New York City. Every possible courtesy will be extended to all visitors.

WM. DEMUTH & CO., New York
World's Largest Makers of Fine Pipes

A 1950 advertisement by William Demuth & Company, then the world's largest pipe maker, featured a thirty-two-inch sculpted pipe depicting Christopher Columbus's landing in the New World. Demuth is credited with popularizing the wooden statue of an Indian chief as a symbol for tobacco stores. The firm was eventually taken over by the Kaywoodie Company. Kaywoodie Company

A distinguishing feature of the Medico was a filter made of absorbent, replaceable paper.

Competition between Kaywoodie and Medico ended in March 1955 when Kaywoodie and its subsidiaries were acquired by S. M. Frank. Expansion continued with the purchase of the New Jersey Briar Pipe Company in 1956 and formation of Medico Pipes (Canada), Ltd., the next year. In the early 1960s another subsidiary (KYM Europe) was created in Livorno, Italy, to distrubute Medico products in Europe, Africa, and the Middle East.

In 1966 the firm developed a synthetic material—Brylon—as a cheaper alternative to briar. A resin mixed at high temperature with wood flour, it proved to be heavier in the mouth than briar and hotter when smoked quickly. But it was resistant to cracking, chipping, charring, and burnout. The company claims to have sold millions and continues to offer this briar alternative.

With headquarters located fifty miles north of New York City in Peekskill, S. M. Frank & Company produces Kaywoodie, Yello-Bole, and Medico, as well as private-label pipes, in Tampa, Florida.

THE KIRSTEN: "THE WORLD'S COOLEST PIPE"

A third pipe maker with an idea as to how to deal with the problem of moisture and still get consistently cool smoke came up with a radical approach: It unified the pipe's shank and stem in a manner that would permit interchanging them with the bowl, and it made them from metal.

Offhand, you might not expect that a radical type of pipe would be invented by a man who had devised a wind tunnel for testing aerodynamics, air-washing equipment for factories, an air-cooled bed, and a propeller that permits boats to stop and turn on a dime. But when German-born Professor F. K. Kirsten was told by his doctor to switch from cigarettes to a pipe, the aeronautical engineer quickly encountered that bane of all pipe smokers—accumulated moisture that found its way to the mouth.

Determined to design a pipe that would eliminate the problem, he devised the "Radiator" stem. Made today of a single piece of ultra-light aerospace-quality aluminum, it allows only clean, cool, moisture-free smoke to pass to the mouth. The stem is fixed to the bowl by means of a screw-on device. This allows the stem to be connected to a wide variety of bowl shapes and sizes made of Mediterranean briar. Stems are available as quarter and full bents, or straight. Bowl styles are called billiard, bulldog, Mandarin, dynasty, Columbus, and brandy. Finishes are offered in silvertone, brasstone, and satin black. Ebonite mouthpieces are black, gray, or bronze, and are offered straight or bent. Buyers who purchase through the firm's catalog are invited to design their own pipes from the pieces available. Prices in a 1997 catalog ranged from $33 for the Jewel to the Designer, a large black-satin-finished stem with an extra-large Turkish block meerschaum bowl for $136. The company remains a family-operated enterprise in Seattle, Washington.

OTHER PIPES

While briar-pipe makers looked for ways to handle the wetness problem, naturally absorbent pipes remained available:

CLAY

Among the leading names in clay production are: Lepeltier, selling directly to the consumer from its factory in Vermont; John Pollock & Company, founded in 1879, producing clays from original molds; and Zenith, a Dutch firm making more than seven million pipes a year.

MEERSCHAUM

If you're buying a pipe with a bowl purportedly lined or made entirely with meerschaum, be wary. Some meerschaum is not hewn from a block of "sea foam" but made of a compound of meerschaum particles and other materials. Here are some reliable sources:

M&L Trading Company
9243 North Keller Avenue
Skokie, IL 60076

Pipes Unlimited
152 Madison Avenue
New York, NY 10016

Royal Meerschaum Pipe Company
Box 9
San Marcos, CA 92069

Ural Pipes
White Bowl, Inc.
225 Berkshire Circle West
Longwood, FL 32750

Meerschaum Importers

Ben-Sim Company
P.O. Box 5742
Bethesda, MD 20814

CAO Meerschaum
830 Kendall Drive
Nashville, TN 37209

London Meerschaum, Ltd.
P.O. Box 1
Cowbridge, South Glamorgan
CF7 7AB, United Kingdom

CORNCOB

Several brands of corncob pipes are marketed—and you can even make one yourself—but if it's America's unique style of pipe that interests you, you won't court disappointment if it's a Missouri Meerschaum.

PROPRIETARY PIPES

Most tobacconists are likely to sell pipes under their own name. Many of these are actually made by major manufacturers and can prove to be sound purchases. Ask the store proprietor about them, with attention to whether they are sold with a guarantee of satisfaction.

Some tobacconists are also pipe makers. A prime example is Peretti's in Boston. Established in 1870 by Libero Joseph Peretti and continued by his heirs, the firm's craftsmen gained fame and followers with beautiful fine-grained freehands carved from Macedonian briar, along with an extensive line of traditional styles.

The Pipe as Gift

Setting out to purchase a pipe as a gift for a veteran pipe smoker without him at your side is venturing where angels fear to tread.

An observer of pipe smoking in the nineteenth century claimed that much might be deduced about a man's character from the way he smokes his pipe. His analysis (perhaps tongue in cheek) may be of value as you go about buying a pipe as a gift:

> The smoker who sends forth smoke from both corners of the mouth in two divergent puffs is crochety and hard to get along with though he may have good mental faculties. The man who after lighting his pipe holds it not only between teeth and lips but with his hand is fastidious and possessed of much personal pride. Such a

smoker will often remove the pipe and examine the bowl to see if it is burning evenly and steadily. Such actions indicate carefulness, sagacity and a character worthy of confidence and esteem.

Men of quick, vivacious temper hardly touch the bit of their pipe to their mouth when, after taking two or three whiffs, they remove it and hold it in their hand in absent-minded fashion. They are men who change their opinions and ambitions often and require the spur of novelty to make them exert their best powers.

The smoker who grips his pipe so firmly between his teeth that marks are left on the mouthpiece is mettlesome, of quick, nervous temper and likes to be tenacious of his opinions one way or the other.

The pipe held so that it hangs somewhat toward the chin indicates the listless, ambitionless person who might stand up to such responsibilities as come to him but would never seek them or strive for high place.

The man who fills his pipe slowly and methodically and smokes mechanically and regularly is likely to be reserved, prudent and a good and dependable friend, while not of a showy exterior.

Unless a gift buyer has made a similar study of the smoker who is to receive the pipe, it's probably better to give one of the accessories described in chapter 7.

As for buying tobacco as a gift, you should also know what you are doing.

ACROSTIC

To thee, blest weed, whose sovereign wiles,
O'er cankered care bring radiant smiles.
Best gift of Love to mortals given!
At once the bud and bliss of Heaven!
Crownless are kings uncrowned by thee;
Content the serf in thy sweet liberty,
O charm of life! O foe of misery!

—Anonymous

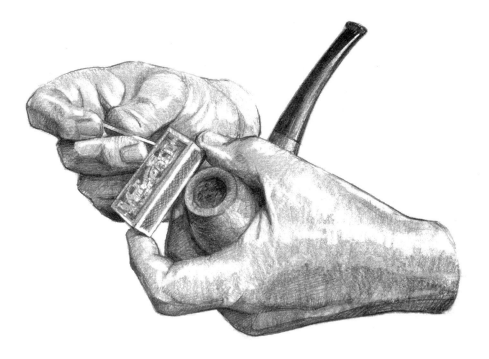

6

Put This in Your Pipe

Let poets rhyme of what they will,
Youth, Beauty, Love, or Glory, still
My theme shall be Tobacco!

—THOMAS JONES

No one can say if Adam and Eve, while blissfully exploring the Garden of Eden, found among the fresh flora a precursor of the plant discovered by natives of the Western Hemisphere and then carried to the rest of the world by Columbus's sailors and those of other nations who followed them. What is not at issue is how fervently people everywhere not only embraced tobacco, but also hailed it as nothing less than a gift of a beneficent deity, or at least the blessing of a bounteous Nature.

Types of Tobacco

Whether the world got tobacco from God or through evolution, evidently one kind of plant was deemed not enough. Botanists have counted more than fifty species of *Nicotiana*. But only two have been grown for commercial use: *Nicotiana rustica* is grown mainly in the Eastern Hemisphere; *Nicotiana tabacum* is found in North and Central America. Called "ordinary tobacco," the latter is the source for all kinds of smoking.

"The basic leaves used in the modern manufacture of pipe tobaccos look and taste so different from one another that it is hard to imagine they all began from the same seed," wrote Mary McNeil in "Selecting Pipe Tobacco" in the "Pipesmoke" section of the Summer 1997 *Smoke* magazine. "They have adapted to the different climates and soils of the world and have been subjected to varied curing methods that give each a unique flavor range."

Kinds of Tobacco

Virginia (also called Bright): This tobacco comes not only from the land of Raleigh, Rolfe, and Pocahontas, but also from North and South Carolina, Georgia, and Florida. It delivers to the smoker a subtle sweetness and somewhat delicate fruity taste. One writer described the experience as "rather tangy and pleasant on the palate, reminiscent of a mild salsa . . . that is zesty at light up and then turns richer as the tobacco is smoked." Virginia is a basic ingredient of a wide range of blends.

Maryland: With a rich brown coloring and bland flavor, this increases the burning properties of other tobaccos. A favorite in the blending of pipe tobaccos by the Swiss, Germans, and French.

Burley: Mainly the product of Tennessee, Kentucky, and Ohio, this is extremely light-tasting and is readily mixed with aromatics. Derived from the White Burley discovered by an Ohio grower, George Webb, in 1864, it is rich and nutty in flavor and ideal for blending with stronger tobaccos, such as Latakia, Perique, and Turkish (below).

Cavendish: An all-encompassing name for Virginia tobacco. Flavored with sugar, rum, and maple, it is repeatedly pressed and heated in order to darken its color.

Latakia: Almost black in color and grown primarily in the north of Syria, this provides a rich and heavy flavor.

Perique: Exceedingly strong—so much so that only the truly brave smoker would try it by itself—this unique American tobacco is grown only in the St. James Parish of Louisiana. As a mixer it brings to a blend an even-burning nature and distinct flavor and aroma.

Turkish: These tobaccos of the East are also called Oriental.

In discussing the transformation of *N. tabacum* into pipe tobacco, Jerome E. Brooks wrote in *The Mighty Leaf,* "Tobacco may seem a tough, rank weed to some, but its nature is fragile and it demands a kind of brooding care."

Cultivation and Harvesting

Like all life, tobacco begins as seeds. Planted in January, February, or March, they germinate best in heavy clay soil that has been painstakingly harrowed, plowed, and fertilized. Once the seedlings have sprung up, they are transplanted at precise intervals. This assures each plant ample space to grow uncrowded by others. When a plant produces ten to fifteen leaves the bottom-most are removed, along with the blossoms. This pruning, called "topping," allows the more desirable middle leaves to flourish in terms of size and body. The plants are left to thrive unmolested for thirty to forty days before the leaves are harvested for curing.

How much tobacco is grown in a season is regulated by the U.S. government as part of the program for subsidizing growers that has become a perennial target of the antismoking movement.

Curing

The collection of leaves that are to become pipe tobacco is carried out in August or September. The way the leaves are cut depends on the method by which they will be cured (dried). There are two processes: air and flue.

In air-curing the leaves are simply allowed to dry by the natural process of evaporation.

Flue-curing uses radiant heat conducted by pipes (flues) from a furnace in a manner similar to heating buildings.

The curing method that is employed depends on the regional characteristics of the tobacco and the desires of the tobacco manufacturer in regard to flavor and aroma.

Virginia is flue-cured. Burley is air-dried in open barns for up to two months. Latakia is smoke-cured over wood fires in a way similar to smoking hams. Powerful Perique is aged much like whiskey, in oaken barrels.

With the curing completed, the leaves are graded and sorted by color and texture and then bundled for shipping to tobacco whole-salers.

The Tobacco Auction

For three decades before the present antismoking movement suc-ceeded in revoking the right of tobacco manufacturers to advertise their wares on radio and television, untallied millions of Americans became familiar with one of the most colorful characters in Ameri-can history—the tobacco auctioneer.

Featured in commercials for Lucky Strike cigarettes, made by the American Tobacco Company, "Speedy Riggs" was a genuine auc-tioneer whose machine-gun-tongued stream of escalating numbers sounded like the babbling of a mad accountant with marbles in his mouth as tobacco buyers made their bids. Speedy's rapid-fire perfor-mance always ended with a blaring triumphal exclamation, "Sold . . . *American.*"

This entertaining sales pitch was not a creature of the imagina-tion of a Madison Avenue advertising agency. Tobacco auctions work that way. Bidders roam through giant warehouses rich with the aroma of tobacco leaves awaiting inspection in row after row of piles and sometimes in large, brimming baskets. Flue-cured Virginia leaf reaches the market from midsummer to midautumn. Burley goes to auction between November and February.

Making Pipe Tobacco

Shipped from auction warehouses to manufacturers in the United States and abroad, the tobacco leaves must be cleaned and refined.

While a large part of the tobacco-manufacturing process has been taken over by mechanization, removal of stems and other undesirable materials remains a highly labor-intensive procedure. Because the bundles arrive in extremely dry condition, a system of moisture replenishment is required to restore suppleness so that the leaves can be handled without being ruined.

It is also at this stage that U.S. manufacturers may elect to introduce nontobacco substances to retain moisture and to add flavorings and sweeteners that have proved popular with American pipe smokers. This flavor-enhancing procedure is called "casing." The tobaccos that result are known as "aromatics."

Tobaccos from England, where addition of flavorings is not permitted by law, are classified, naturally, as "English."

Mixing and Blending

Like most whiskeys, pipe tobaccos go through a blending procedure in which two or more types of tobacco are mixed to achieve a manufacturer's desired flavor and aroma, much the way a chef prepares a gourmet dinner.

Tobacco Cutting

Leaves for pipe tobacco may be cut in four ways:

Ribbon (also called English, shag, and long cut): This is fine and stringy and usually a blend of Virginia and Cavendish.

Cube (also known as chop cut): Very thick, it is generally a Burley.

Flake: Cut into irregular pieces that smoke fast.

Plug: Soaked in honey, this is a chunk of tobacco that is molded under pressure and looks something like a candy bar. This is the tobacco through which Mark Twain and generations of Americans learned the delights of the pipe. It is cut with a pocketknife into the proper size and shape to fit into a pipe. It can also be chewed. Also known as cake.

Packaging

While pipe tobacco packed in large or pocket-size tins remains a popular choice for buyers, the tin is rivaled by the pocket-size, paper, water- and airtight pouch containing about an ounce. These handy packages make it easy and less costly for the adventuresome pipe smoker to test the broad variety of tobaccos available, whether aromatic or naturally aged.

Among the most popular mass-market brands have been Sail, whose three varieties come in different-colored packs: Borkum Riff, with pouches featuring either a coat of arms or a drawing of a tri-masted ship with sails down and flags flying; Captain Black, which also uses a nautical motif; Flying Dutchman; Cherry Blend; Edgeworth; Walnut; Bond Street; Mixture #79; Balkan Sobranie; MacBarren; Holiday; Prince Albert, named for Queen Victoria's son "Bertie," Prince of Wales, who became King Edward VII and also had a brand of cigars named after him; and, of course, Sir Walter Raleigh.

Recommending exploration of the universe of choices in pipe tobaccos, Mary McNeil wrote, "Discovering the subtle and interesting flavors of the full range of pipe tobaccos available from the different manufacturers is great fun, as many pleasant smoking experiences will be found, and fond memories created, on the road to that elusive perfect blend."

Should the large number of packaged tobaccos prove unsatisfying, the pipe smoker may find exactly what he's looking for in special mixtures offered through catalogs by mail-order firms.

The perfect blend also might be found at a neighborhood tobacco shop offering both the proprietor's special blends and an oppportunity for the smoker to come up with his own recipe. Patrons of the historic L. J. Peretti's in Boston, for instance, have found for sale an assortment of store blends ranging from a "Boston's Best Cavendish" to Black Virginia, Burlington Blend, Cherry Cavendish, Whiskey Cavendish, Ebony, Tropical Fruit, Irish-Mist, and Ultra-Lite. For do-it-yourselfers the choice (by ounce or pound) might be: Virginia long cut or flake, fire-cured and Golden Cavendish, Kentucky and White Burley, two kinds of Turkish, Latakia, Perique, various flakes, and even cigar leaf.

Imported tobaccos include the Dunhill Line, Sobranie, Three Nuns, St. Bruno Flake, Erinmore, Edgeworth, Esoterica, Ashton, Rattray's, McClelland, McConnell, and Wessex assortments.

A New Yorker who ventures off the Avenue of the Americas at Rockefeller Center and into De La Concha might choose a tin of what the tobacconist calls its "Renowned Blends," with exotic names such as Khartoum and Barbados Gold. "Our Pop-

Old tobacco tins preserved at Boston's historic Peretti's tobacco store, arranged according to type of tobacco. © Kevin Gordon

Tobacco being mixed and weighed by Robert Peretti. The antique scale was designed for use by nineteenth-century metal assayers to measure gold.
© Kevin Gordon

ular" blends range from Classic Burley to Tropical Mist, Swiss Mocha, Marabella, and the irresistibly romantic-sounding Black Magic, Buccaneer, Treasure Chest, Pieces-of-Eight, Turkish Delight, Paradise, and Warhorse.

Customers of Iwan Ries & Company of Chicago find the venerable tobacconist offering its own "Three Star" selection of aromatics named for colors: Blue, Gray, Bronze, Red, Green, and Gold, as well as aromatic and nonaromatic "IRC Traditional Blends."

Dunhill in the world's major cities offers round tins of the firm's unique Nightcap, My Mixture 965, Royal Yacht, Early Morning Pipe, and Standard Mixture Medium.

In whatever form pipe tobacco might be offered, whether packaged by a mass-marketer or concocted by a local tobacconist, the novice or veteran pipe smoker is certain to appreciate J. B. Priestley's assertion: "Opening a new tin of tobacco is one of the lasting small pleasures of life."

MOTTO FOR A TOBACCO JAR

Come! don't refuse sweet Nitcotina's aid,
  But woo the goddess through a yard of clay,
And soon you'll own she is the fairest maid
  To stifle pain, and drive old Care away.
Nor deem it waste; and what though to ash she burns,
If for your outlay you get good returns.
                                        —Anonymous

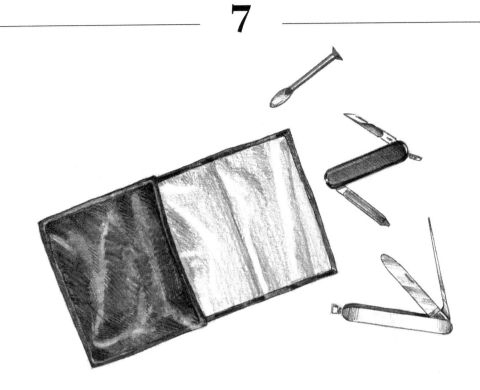

7

Pouches, Jars, Racks, Reamers, Tampers, and Other Gadgetry

Pipe smoking is the most protracted of all forms of tobacco consumption. It may explain why pipe smokers are regarded as patient men—and philosophers.

—JEROME E. BROOKS
The Mighty Leaf

"The fully equipped pipe smoker, often a very earnest connoisseur about his habit, is busiest of all those who enjoy tobacco," Brooks continued. "His pipe must be cleaned, the bowl filled, pressed and examined before lighting; the pouch must be replaced, the tobacco lighted and relighted and relighted. Thus the hand and the eye play an added part in the use of the sedentary pipe."

This cannot be said of the two other options available to the individual who chooses to smoke. The only accoutrement you need to smoke a cigarette or a cigar is a means of lighting it. (Those who smoke premium cigars will also want an end-trimmer.)

But the pipe smoker requires an array of special equipment. This is why the humorist Robert Benchley advised that one must never hire a pipe smoker, because he will be too busy fiddling with his pipe and trying to light it and keep it lit to get any work done.

The apparatus of pipe smoking serves two purposes:

1. To keep the tobacco fresh.
2. To maintain the pipe's smokability.

Things to Keep Your Tobacco Fresh

How to maintain your pipe tobacco's freshness depends on how you buy it, whether in bulk or a little at a time. If it's the former you'll need something to preserve its long-term moistness. There are two ways to go.

THE HUMIDOR OR JAR

Also necessary for a cigar smoker who keeps a large supply at hand, the humidor is an airtight container with a built-in device that provides a constant measure of moisture. It can be no more than a sponge. Some cigar-storage boxes can hold hundreds of cigars, even a thousand, and have a complex unit with a gauge to register humidity within. Tobacconists have walk-in humidors, as do some individuals with the financial wherewithal to afford to build a special climate-controlled room.

Pipe-tobacco humidors are more likely to be in the form of a canister or jar with a lid containing a material (a piece of sponge or absorbent clay) for holding a moisturizing agent such as water. The moisture is kept inside (and odors are sealed out) by a gasket between the canister or jar and its cover. Some pipe smokers prefer to slip in a chunk of apple or a bit of orange or lemon peel. Others like to add a splash or two of rum or brandy.

Unlike cigar humidors, which are wooden boxes, pipe-tobacco canisters and jars come in an amazing variety of styles, from a simple glass model that could just as easily store candy or nuts to works of sculptive art. These are often in the form of busts, of which one of the most common is Sherlock Holmes. Others offer pirates, old-time sailors, birds, and heads of dogs and horses.

On the subject of the tobacco jar an unknown writer left us this poetic pun:

> *Keep me at hand; and as my fumes arise,*
> *You'll find* ajar *the gates of Paradise.*

The earthly place for the tobacco jar is in the home or the office. For the pipe smoker on the go there is a portable moisture conserver that slips nicely into a coat pocket.

THE POUCH

Holding about one ounce of tobacco, the pouch is commonly available in three styles:

Roll-up: Resembling a man's wallet or a woman's small purse and made of leather, plastic, or cloth, this has a pocket at one end and a long foldable flap.

Zippered top: Also shaped like a wallet or purse, it closes with a zipper and is usually made of leather.

Round: This pouch looks a little like an ice bag, or one of the sacks holding coins that you see in movies about pirates or other quaintly costumed characters.

Manufacturers of the most popular pipe-tobacco brands make their products available in roll-up plastic-lined paper pouches that serve very well to keep the contents fresh. You can also transfer tobacco from the paper pouch to your own. Or you can tuck the entire paper pouch inside your classier leather one.

Although Sherlock Holmes is known to have kept pipe tobacco in the toe of a Persian slipper, Watson recorded that Holmes's mantel held "a litter of pipes [and] tobacco-pouches." And while the good doctor did not note whether Holmes also had an assortment of pipe tools, it is elementary to deduce that if he had pouches, he also possessed other accompaniments to enhance the act of pipe smoking, whether mulling over a case in the Baker Street rooms or leaping into the last hansom from the hack line and racing across London in the cause of whatever game was afoot.

Gadgets to Keep Your Pipe Working

These objects, which every pipe smoker needs, are guaranteed to set off the metal detectors at airports and in other places where we used to go before the dawn of the era of terrorism. And a few of them could cause those who are uninitiated into the world of pipes to wonder if *you* might be intent on unleashing some kind of mischief.

THE TAMPER

It's a piece of metal with a round, flat end that is used to press down tobacco. Some also come with a shaft that is pointed (making it ideal for cleaning under fingernails) and edged like a blade for scraping the pipe bowl. Some have the tamper on one end and a dottle scooper on the other.

Lacking a metal tamper, you can employ the end of a pen, but only if it's made of metal. And, as was suggested earlier with a warning about painful consequences, there's always your finger.

THE PIPE SMOKER'S COMPANION

Certainly no pipe gadget looks more like a devilish device, or a plaything from a sadist's toy box, than this handy little metal tool. Small enough to fit snugly in a vest pocket, it consists of a poker, spoon, and tamper held together by a ring. Some also have a retractable blade similar to a pocketknife. The poker is for unclogging the pipe's airways. The spoon is for scooping out dottle and scraping bowls, as is the knife blade. The tamper is for, well . . . tamping.

REAMER

Shaped like a cross with a rounded wing top and a shaft whose tip is rounded to fit the bottom of a bowl, this device also resembles something thought up by the hooded master of an Inquisition torture chamber. When inserted into the bowl of a pipe, the shaft is a two-sided scraper. But the shaft also has a hinged blade that remains undeployed until the device is turned clockwise. This raises the second blade and turns the gadget into a four-sided reamer that scrapes cake evenly. It's effective, until you have to get the dottle out of the heel, because, quite inexplicably, this otherwise very clever tool does not come with a built-in scoop.

PIPE CLEANERS

Long, thin wires with bristles that can be cottony soft or as rough as a scouring brush, these are used for getting the gunk out of the pipe's airways. (They also prove ideal for tying things, such as the tops of plastic garbage bags if you misplace the fasteners that come with the bags.) Available in two styles: blunt on both ends or with one end tapered.

Indispensable, they were once the cheapest part of smoking a pipe. Not anymore! In 1997 a package of the most popular brand, Dill's, cost as much as a package of machine-made cigars or one moderately priced premium cigar.

The only consumable accoutrement of pipe smoking that seems to have gone up more in price than a bundle of pipe cleaners is a box of wooden matches. (The cost of tobacco is excluded because the principal cause of the rise in tobacco prices has been the imposition of punishing taxation by federal, state, and local governments, goaded into action by their own greed and political pressure from the minions of the smoke police.)

Should a fresh pipe cleaner be left in the stem and shank when a pipe is resting? The experts' consensus is yes.

They also concur on the best way to store pipes.

Pipe Racks

Second only to a necktie rack as a project for teenage boys in wood shop classes in junior high school, the pipe rack is a prime example of "form following function."

The design is simple: a top with holes in it, something to to support the top, and a base. Size depends on how many pipes are to go into it. Height is dictated by the length of the pipes. Designs range from one- and two-pipe holders, ideal for cradling a pipe or a brace of them on a table next to your favorite chair, to those that hold six, eight, a dozen, or more. Some arrange the pipes in two or more tiers. The most common material is wood, but holders are also available in porcelain and other ceramics. "There are few more satisfying things," wrote Carl Weber in *The Pleasures of Pipe Smoking,* "than a row of pipes ranged in a rack, but a pipe rack also serves a utilitarian purpose by insisting that the pipe stand upright."

The objective is to allow drainage of moisture from bowl, shank, and stem. But you can get an argument as to whether a pipe should go into a rack with the bowl at the top or at the bottom. Georges Herment insisted the pipe be inverted—that is, stored with the bowl up. Weber, Hacker, this author, and most experts on this side of the Atlantic, including the rack makers, believe the pipe should rest bowl-down.

Another attraction of the rack is that it allows the proud owner of the pipes to display them, if not for the pleasure of others, then for himself alone.

As Georges Herment wrote, "A pipe can be enjoyed without so much as its being lit."

THE SMOKER'S CALENDAR

When January's cold appears.
A glowing pipe my spirit cheers;
And still it glads the length'ning day
'Neath February's milder sway.
When March's keener winds succeed,
What charms me like the burning weed
When April mounts the solar car,
I join him, puffing a cigar;
And May, so beautiful and bright,
Still finds the pleasing weed alight.
To balmy zephyrs it gives zest
When June in gayest livery's drest.
Through July, Flora's offspring smile,
But still Nicotia's can beguile;
And August, when its fruits are ripe,
Matures my pleasure in a pipe.
September finds me in the garden,
Communing with a long churchwarden.
Even in the wine of dull October
I smoke my pipe and sip my "robar."
November's soaking show'rs require
The smoking pipe and blazing fire.
The darkest day in drear December's—
That's lighted by their glowing embers.

—Anonymous

8

When and Where

A pipe, a book,
   A cosy nook,
A fire—at least its embers;
   A dog, a glass:—
   'Tis thus we pass
Such hours as one remembers.

—ANONYMOUS

efore the cigarette came to be the dominant way of smoking in the twentieth-century United States there was a time when the male rite of passage of going away to college included taking up pipe smoking. To the "collegiate" between the world wars a pipe was as much a part of campus life as a straw hat and raccoon coat. When time came for saying good-byes it was likely to be a sentimental moment enfused with a good deal of smoke, such as in this old college song:

Englishmen whose wives would not permit smoking in their homes found boon companionship in coffeehouses where proprietors happily provided pipes, tobacco, and bracing drinks.
New York Public Library

Come, seniors, come and fill your pipes,
   Your richest incense raise;
Let's take a smoke, a parting smoke,
   For good old by-gone days!

While the pipe as masculine bonder became part of American college campuses in the years after the World War I, its debut as a central component of men-only sociability came in latter years of the 1600s as tobacco became popular in England. Married men with wives who allowed no smoking in their houses had three choices. They could not smoke, leave the house and light up in the outdoors, or persuade their wives to allow them a space in the house (or in its immediate proximity) in which smoking would be permitted. These became a feature of many homes and were known as "smoking rooms." Because some had stone floors (for safety) they were also called "stone parlors."

Men who did not have the good fortune to have a place of their own for smoking soon found hospitable locales removed from their homes in the form of coffeehouses. In the *Spectator* (No. 568) Charles Addison wrote of what it was like in a coffeehouse in 1714: "I was yesterday in a coffee-house not far from the Royal Exchange, where I observed three persons in close conference over a pipe of tobacco; upon which, having filled one for my own use, I lighted it at the little wax candle that stood before them; and after having thrown in two or three whiffs amongst them, sat down and made one of the company. I need not tell my reader, that lighting a man's pipe at the same candle is looked upon among brother-smoakers as an overture to conversation and friendship."

For males only, these coffeehouses were the forerunners of the men's clubs that developed in England, especially in London and in the university cities of Oxford and Cambridge. The passing of centuries did not quench the practice. An Oxford student wrote in 1858 that the university's men were "rather particular about the pipes they smoked," preferring a French brand called Fiolet, Saint Omer, "made of soft clay that easily coloured."

The Alfred Club, founded in 1808, was described by Lord Byron as "a little too sober and literary, perhaps, but, on the whole, a decent resource on a rainy day."

Around 1842, Tennyson visited the Old Crock in London and had "a beefsteak, a potato, a cut of cheese, a pint of port, and afterwards a pipe." But the pipe enjoyed most by Tennyson was the first of the day, which he lit up immediately after breakfast.

Scottish author Kenneth Grahame wrote in 1898 that a morning pipe "comes to unjaded senses like the kiss of one's first love."

Countless pipe smokers concurred then and agree today.

When to Smoke a Pipe

An early rhymist thought anytime is right:

A pipe at nine
Is always fine.
A puff at noon
Is none too soon.
A pipe at three
The thing for me.
A pipe at seven
An aroma to heaven.
A pipe at nine
Is half divine.

A pipe before slumber
Makes just the right number.

Even the paradigm of pipe smokers, Sherlock Holmes, varied his choice of pipe according to time of day, filling the bowls of briars and clays as his mood dictated with pinches of the strong tobacco that he kept in the toe of a Persian slipper on the fireplace mantel. (Author's note: not recommended!)

Pipe Accompaniments

Aficionados of the form of tobacco that Columbus and his sailors found natives smoking in the West Indies insist that the ideal conclusion to a fine meal can only be a cigar. Not so. An after-dinner pipe provides an equally delightful experience, no matter what was on the menu.

A pipe is also a superb companion when drinking, whether it is a snifter of brandy or glass of Scotch, bourbon, or other spirit. It goes well with wine, a mug of beer, or a cup of coffee or tea. And, of course, it's fine all by itself.

Like a cigar, a pipe can be a boon companion whether you are with one or two friends, in the midst of a throng, or alone.

But what a pipe offers a smoker that a cigar does not is the almost infinite variety of sizes, shapes, weight, colors, and textures of the material from which it's made—briar or other wood, clay, the gourd of the calabash, meerschaum, or even stone. There is also a huge selection of tobaccos, natural or blended, aromatic or not.

Another difference between smoking a cigar and a pipe is in the fact that while a cigar has differing lengths, thicknesses, and particular properties of leaves used for fillers, binders, and wrappers, to paraphrase Gertude Stein on the topic of roses, a cigar is a cigar is a cigar.

But there is a diversity in pipes that lets you choose one on the basis of what you will be doing while smoking it. Pipes alone can be selected to suit and enhance particular activities.

Carl Weber proposed that if a pipe is to be smoked while reading, a long-stemmed one will keep smoke from getting in the eyes. For those who smoke while working with both hands, such as while typing or using a computer, the curved stem is better because it is the easiest to hold in your teeth. The same is true for smoking while going on walks. Smoking outdoors while hunting or fishing proves most satisfying if the pipe is a rugged one: a cherrywood or corncob. Small bowls are ideal for intermissions at the theater or opera. A big pipe on the order of a calabash suits the contemplative evening hours spent at home.

Finally, if a smoker has to keep a close watch on his tobacco budget, no method of smoking proves more economical in the long term than a pipe.

Where to Smoke a Pipe

Before the antismoking movement succeeded in enactment of strict legislation mandating when and where smoking of any kind is allowed, the following guidelines had been laid out by Carl Weber in *The Pleasures of Pipe Smoking:*

1. Never smoke where there is a sign warning you it is prohibited in that place.

2. Don't smoke in any public place where you can sense or see it is annoying anybody.

3. Don't smoke in an elevator.

4. Don't smoke when you are part of a dense crowd.

5. Always ask permission to smoke when you are a guest.

6. Always ask permission of a lady who is *your* guest.

7. Never empty the burned-out tobacco [dottle] into a tiny ashtray. Never spill it anywhere,

8. Don't tap your pipe or knock it against some other object, nervously wave it when you talk, or use it [in] any way that may distract from somebody else's talk. Remember that the pipe is a symbol of harmony, pleasure, amity, and even peace— so handle and use it gracefully.

9. Be alert to the one real danger of pipe smoking—the possibility of burning ashes setting something afire.

In sum: When you feel like smoking, be courteous and show the wisdom that everyone expects of a pipe smoker.

But don't be cowed by today's shrill smoke police, nor be taken in by the propaganda of those who are determined to race headlong from a rather courteous position of recent years (when the anti-smoking claque invented the catchphrase "Thank-you for not smoking") to outright prohibition of all smoking. In pursuit of this goal they have coined a fresh slogan to paint on their banners as they march toward their utopia, namely, "A smoke-*free* America." For a nation that offers the most freedom in the world it's a phrase that is both moronic and *oxy*moronic.

The Health Police

When the merry old soul of a nursery rhyme, Old King Cole, called for his pipe and bowl, nobody in his court had either the temerity or the daring to raise a voice in protest about possible ill effects of his smoking on himself and others in the dubious form of "second-hand smoke."

As has been shown, since Raleigh's time tobacco has always had naysayers to denounce it as a "stinking weed" and try to do all within their power to stamp it out, from brutal taxation to restrictive legislation. When all else failed there were icy glares and crude epithets directed at smokers by the health-and-fitness activists and from tobacco abolitionists who, like their misguided ancestors who tried to take alcoholic drinks out of Americans' hands, can't stand the idea that someone finds happiness in the produce of the earth. For those who sought to stamp out drinking, the enemy had been the distillation of barley, corn, and other grains. Now it's tobacco's turn.

In the current phase of the long war against smoking the primary target of the smoke police is cigarettes, and the weapon is the allegation that tobacco is a menace to health.

Do cigarettes make some people sick? Sure. Do they render *all* who smoke them ill? Obviously not. If cigarette smoking were the cause of cancer and the host of other diseases attributed to it, everybody who smokes cigarettes would come down with one or all such maladies. They all don't.

But even if it could be proved that cigarettes are bad for everyone's health, what about pipe smoking?

While U.S. surgeons general have condemned all types of smoking, the first *Smoking and Health* (Public Health Service Publication No. 1103, page 112) noted, "Death rates for current pipe smokers are *little if at all higher* [emphasis added] than for nonsmokers even with men smoking 10 pipefuls per day and with men who had smoked pipes for more than 30 years."

The same surgeon general's report stated on page 92 that pipe smokers who inhale live just as long as nonsmokers, and that pipe smokers who *don't* inhale live *longer* than nonsmokers (with a death rate 20 percent lower than nonsmokers').

In speculating on why this was so in *The Pleasures of Pipe Smoking,* Carl Weber opined that the pipe smoker was likely to be less susceptible to the ills that befall some cigarette smokers: high concentrations of nicotine absorption as a result of inhaling tobacco smoke, frequency of smoking, and the psychological makeup of the smoker. He correctly pointed out that in contrast to the cigarette smoker, who generally consumes a large number of cigarettes per day, the pipe smoker—even one who has his pipe going constantly—burns far less tobacco, and at a considerably slower rate, *without inhaling.* And because pipe tobacco does not deliver as much nicotine as cigarettes, the result is a dramatically lower intake. In addition, none of the additives that go into making cigarettes go into pipe tobacco.

There is also evidence cited in *Smoking and Health* that the psychological nature of the smoker may have something to do with why one person chooses cigarettes while another picks a pipe. In noting that people smoke cigarettes to relieve tension and nervousness, the report asked, "Is smoking merely an expression of tension, or does it serve as a reducer of psychic tension?"

As discovered in the research by Burton Shean cited in chapter 3 of this book, cigarette smokers described themselves as "lively" personalities who prefer taking action to planning action, are happiest when taking part in something that calls for rapid action, and are inclined to be quick-acting. This is the individual whom psychologists categorize as a "Type A" personality. Such a smoker may be expected to smoke a great deal, if for no other reason than to relieve boredom and stress, or out of sheer nervousness.

There is also a sedative side to nicotine, which could explain why someone who smokes cigarettes and has finished making love feels a need to light up.

And whether seeking a quick boost or the relaxation afforded by nicotine, the cigarette smoker must *inhale*.

Pipe smokers not only don't inhale, they also fall into the "Type B" personality classification. As the 1973 Criswell study found, pipe smokers are calm, stable, pensive, internalized, and lacking in anxiety. And, as has been shown, the process of smoking a pipe requires both deliberation and slowness of action in order to savor its tactile pleasures—the feel of the pipe, the eddying plumes of smoke drifting from the mouth, and the pleasure of the taste of tobacco, which can be experienced not by inhaling the smoke, but only by holding it in the mouth. As Dayton Matlick, the editor of *Pipes and Tobaccos* magazine, put it, "Pipe smokers enjoy smoking the same way some people enjoy meditating."

What every such contemplative pipe smoker is certain to come to appreciate is that the best way to get through life is by taking the advice of Aristotle: Be moderate in all things.

It is the virtue of the pipe that its proper enjoyment can be attained *only* by smoking moderately.

"The true pipe smoker is not antic, but observes the laws of good manners, " counseled Carl Weber. "He is worthy of his pipe, for he knows how, where, and when to smoke it."

9

The Delight of the Pipe

*After I learned the delight of the pipe, I suppose
there was no youngster of my age who could more
deftly cut a plug of tobacco as to make it available
for pipe smoking.*

—MARK TWAIN

$\mathcal{F}$ollowing an intolerable lecturing and "pecking" by Miss Watson on Moses, the Good Book, prayers, and living "so as to go to the good place," a fictional boy by the name of Huckleberry Finn saw no advantage in going where the dour Miss Watson would be going. Making up his mind that he would not try for it, he went to his room with a piece of candle, put it on a table, and sat down to try to think of something cheerful.

Instead, Huck accidentally incinerated a wayward spider in the candle flame. Interpreting this act as "an awful bad sign" that would "fetch some bad luck," he reported that he sat again, "a-shaking all over, and got out my pipe for a smoke."

Thus, on the fifth page of his classic novel *Huckleberry Finn,* Mark Twain's immortal portrait of this nineteenth-century barefoot boy with independent intent illuminated what has been called by another writer the "sweet enchantment of solitude" and the "sublime delight" of a pipe.

For John Paul Beaumier and Lewis Camp in *The Pipe Smoker* it was "the exquisite pleasure of puffing." Carl Weber's *The Pleasures of Pipe Smoking* spoke of "a sense of peace and satisfaction." Georges Herment agreed, writing in his book *The Pipe* that pipe smoking "gives the system an equilibrium that is material as well as spiritual."

The latter is what the smoker both brings to the experience and discovers through it. Countless writers have mused on the tobacco as a metaphor for the fragile and transitory nature of the human body. The ash is a visible reminder of Scripture's admonition that God took mankind from the earth and that to the earth all of us shall return; "ashes to ashes, dust to dust." And the rising smoke has been seen as symbolic of the soul making its departure from what Shakespeare termed our "mortal coil" to "that undiscover'd country from whose bourn no traveler returns."

The material aspect is the pipe itself—the look and handling of it in choosing it from the myriad available in the pipe shop, its breaking-in period, and the carrying out of the rituals of smoking it that involve the equipment discussed in the previous chapter. And there is the pipe as a stirrer of memories of happy hours passed while smoking.

It is this traditional view of the pipe smoker as relaxed and con-templative that has been a common theme of advertising by pipe manufacturers and tobacconists.

The Delight of Pipes in Advertising

Through the years pipes have been promoted by innumerable representations of the gentleman at hearthside in slippers and robe. And the comfortable and reassuring figure in many of these ads was a celebrity, preferably a movie actor or, in some instances, a sports per-sonality. One such was the New York Yankees' star and later club man-ager Billy Martin, who appeared in television commercials in the 1980s for Captain Black pipe tobacco.

One of the most inventive ways of advertising pipe tobacco on television was the integration of the sales pitch into the 1950s pro-gram *Martin Kane, Private Eye.* Initially starring the veteran movie actor William Gargan, the title role was taken over successively by Lloyd Nolan and Lee Tracy. Broadcast live a decade before the U.S. surgeon general's report on smoking and health launched the worst antismoking campaign since King James had Sir Walter Raleigh's head chopped off, the drama would each week come to a halt halfway through as Marty found time to set aside his sleuthing to drop in at the neighborhood tobacco shop for conversation with the owner. This chat inevitably got around to the virtues of the show's sponsor's full line of merchandise, including cigarettes, snuff, and chewing

When Jeremy Brett brought Sherlock Holmes to the TV screen (with David Burke as Watson in the first series of programs), the pipes in the detective's hand ran the gamut from clays to this elegant church-warden.
Granada TV

tobacco. Restocked with tobacco for his pipe, Marty departed the store and crime detection resumed.

The Delight of Pipes on Television

Pipe smoking as a delightful experience was also promoted indirectly as bad guys were tracked down on television by rotund, pipe-smoking William Conrad as private eye Frank Cannon. And, of course, there was Sherlock Holmes in a cheaply made series with Ronald Howard (son of Leslie Howard of *Gone with the Wind* fame) as the sleuth of Baker Street (1954), and, impressively faithful to the Conan Doyle stories, Jeremy Brett in the 1980s.

Other small-screen characters who appeared to find delight in pipes were usually the fathers in family situation comedies. These TV dads included Fred MacMurray as widower Stephen Douglas on *My Three Sons* (1960–1965). Between October 1957 and September 1963 it was Hugh Beaumont as Ward Cleaver on *Leave It to Beaver* who kept both his temper and the smoking lamp lit. On the air between 1952 and 1966, *Ozzie and Harriet* featured domestic doings of the real-life Nelson family (Ozzie and Harriet and sons David and nascent rock-and-roll star Ricky). A pipe was likely to be found either in Ozzie's possession or that of neighbor "Thorny" Thornbury, played by the affable Don Defore.

Television newsmen who smoked pipes—though not on the air—included CBS's Walter Cronkite and NBC's John Chancellor.

The Delight of Pipes in Movies

While the Coca-Cola company removed the pipe that Clement Moore's poem had placed in St. Nicholas's mouth, replacing it with a bottle of Coke in Santa's hand, the image of the right jolly old elf as a pipe smoker has endured. More than a century after Moore's famed poem appeared, Hollywood's most famous Kris Kringle shows up on television every Yuletide season in the form of lovable pipe-smoking Edmund Gwenn as Macy's department store's Santa in the original version of the movie *Miracle on Thirty-Fourth Street.*

For moviemakers through the years wishing to convey the immediate impression that a character in a movie was admirable, nothing could beat a pipe. As venerable and wise as white-haired actor Lewis Stone seemed in the role of Mickey Rooney's father in the popular *Andy Hardy* film series, Judge Hardy's fair temperament was rendered indisputable by his pipe. Give a film character a pipe and the audience instantly spotted the good guy. If a director or actor wanted to convey a shady or plain criminal figure, he turned to a cigar. For the nervous and edgy, or just to keep an actor's hands occupied, it was the cigarette.

The same held true for exhibiting anger or anguish, such as Humphrey Bogart's stubbing out of a cigarette as Richard Blaine in *Casablanca* while lamenting that of all the gin joints in all the world Ingrid Bergman walked into his. This was a scene that would have been unplayable had Rick smoked a pipe, as did Bogey when not on screen. Nor could a pipe suit Sam Spade, the hard-boiled private eye of *The Maltese Falcon,* who sent Mary Astor to prison with as much cool as he extinguished his cigarette in an ashtray, an act that a generation of smokers called "Bogeying."

Other personalites who found delight in pipes:

Sparky Anderson: Baseball team manager.

Neil Armstrong: First man to set foot on the moon.

Isaac Asimov: For this author of sci-fi novels and books on almost every other subject, a large briar pipe was as necessary to a brainy image as his large, thick black-rimmed eyeglasses and gray mutton-chop whiskers.

Dan Aykroyd: *Saturday Night Live* alumnus who graduated to the big screen and more than held his own oppposite Jessica Tandy and Morgan Freeman in *Driving Miss Daisy.*

Johann S. Bach: Composer. Clays.

Sir Francis Bacon: English writer, contemporary of Raleigh and Shakespeare.

James M. Barrie: Creator of Peter Pan; also wrote *My Lady Nicotine* (1890), a valentine to smoking.

Alexander Graham Bell: Before he could put down his pipe to take a call, he had to invent the telephone.

Robert Benchley: Humorist of the 1930s and 1940s in print and on screen is said to have come in out of the rain one day and announced, "I must get out of these wet clothes and into a dry martini."

Jim Bowie: Flinty freedom fighter who would never leave home without the huge knife that bears his name, nor without a pipe; smoked his last one at the Alamo.

Abe Burrows: Quick-witted, sharp-tongued producer of *Guys and Dolls* and other Broadway hits of the 1950s.

Richard E. Byrd: To the Arctic explorer a pipe was *really* a hand- and nose-warmer.

George Gordon, Lord Byron: His passion for a pipe didn't keep him from penning the first ode to cigars.

Steven J. Cannell: Omnipresent producer of TV action shows.

Pablo Casals: Cellist, but not while playing.

Casanova: For this randy Italian whose name has become synonymous with womanizing, a pipe was an enduring love.

Bennett Cerf: Founder of Random House, raconteur, and panelist on 1950's television's popular *What's My Line,* whose host, **John Daly,** was also a pipe smoker.

Raymond Chandler: Creator of private eye Philip Marlowe.

Graham Chapman: Of *Monty Python* fame.

John Cheever: Best-selling novelist.

Jacques Cousteau: Not during his renowned, pioneering underwater explorations, of course.

Stephen Crane: Newspaperman and author of the Civil War novel *The Red Badge of Courage* never witnessed a battle up close until he packed his pipes and went to Cuba to cover Teddy Roosevelt's Rough Riders.

Davy Crockett: Frontiersman, congressman, and a hero of the Alamo whose pipe was as much a hallmark as his coonskin hat and buckskin pants.

Hume Cronyn: His wife, Jessica Tandy, and a pipe were constant companions during his long career as Broadway-film-TV actor in more parts than probably even he can recall.

Bing Crosby: The only singer-actor to have a style of pipe named for him.

Peter Cushing: One of life's great mysteries is how a pipe-smoking English gentleman wound up scaring the wits out of audiences in so many horror movies. On the other hand, he also portrayed Sherlock Holmes.

Charles Darwin: He shook the world by contending that human beings are descended from apes. He did so by writing a huge book. But basically the same thing had been said by another Englishman, **Ben Jonson,** who noted, "The pipe marks the point at which the orangutan ends and man begins."

Cecil B. De Mille: Director, producer, writer, and frequent narrator of his own epic movies.

Allan Dulles: Head of the CIA under President Eisenhower, he once took his pipe from his mouth long enough to greet Soviet boss Nikita Khrushchev with, "I've been reading your mail."

Wyatt Earp: But not during the thirty seconds or so that it took him, his brothers, and Doc Holliday to win in the gunfight at Tombstone, Arizona's, O.K. Corral.

Billy Eckstein: When not singing.

Albert Einstein: Fuzzy-haired scientific genius who explained that everything is relative.

Ralph Waldo Emerson: Highly quotable American essayist.

William Faulkner: Kept up the image of writer as pipist.

Barry Fitzgerald: Irish-born character actor, best known as the elderly priest contending with Bing Crosby's warbling "Father O'Malley" in *Going My Way* and as the jaunting cart-driving chaperon for John Wayne and Maureen O'Hara in *The Quiet Man,* but he was also stellar as the pipe-stem-chewing New York City homicide detective in Jules Dassin's gritty film *The Naked City.*

Shelby Foote: Best-selling author and Civil War historian could be the poster boy for the pipe smoker as intellectual.

Edward Fox: Suave Britsh actor, probably best known as the ice-cold assassin-for-hire in *Day of the Jackal*. Also played Edward VIII, the pipe-smoking British monarch who gave up the throne to marry "the woman I love."

Frederick: Same-name kings of Prussia (two) and Denmark.

Sigmund Freud: While some of the followers of the pioneering cigar-smoking Austrian psychiatrist saw a cigar as a phallic symbol, he said, "Sometimes a cigar is just a cigar." He also sought oral gratification from pipes.

Clark Gable: In *Gone with the Wind* as Rhett Butler he smoked cigars, but off screen it was usually a pipe.

Theodor Seuss Geisel: While writing *The Cat in the Hat, The Grinch Who Stole Christmas,* and other fanciful tales for tots.

Arthur Godfrey: Sold Chesterfield cigarettes on radio, but favored a pipe when off the air.

Cary Grant: What else would an English-born gentleman with all that sophistication smoke?

Hugh Hefner: The pipe smoker as playboy.

Lou Holtz: Coach of the Notre Dame football team kept up the tradition of **Knute Rockne** by puffing a pipe as "Fighting Irish" elevens racked up winning seasons.

Edwin Hubble: Astronomer and namesake of the orbiting telescope that searches the universe without its view being obscured by any kind of smoke.

Jeremy Irons: His portrayal of pipe-smoking Charles Ryder in the public-TV production of Evelyn Waugh's *Brideshead Revisted* made the smooth English actor an instant star in America and launched a successful career in movies.

James Joyce: You'll need a lot of pipes to keep you going when you read his massive novel *Ulysses.*

Boris Karloff: Another really nice guy who put down his pipe to terrify movie audiences.

Jerome Kern: Composer whose *Porgy and Bess* (1927), in collaboration with pipe-smoking **Oscar Hammerstein II,** set the standard for all subsequent Broadway musicals.

Charles Lamb: Asked how he got to be such an ardent pipe smoker, he replied, "I toiled after it, sir, as some men toil after virtue."

Sinclair Lewis: American novelist puffed away while skewering 1920s societal norms.

Bela Lugosi: Except while putting the bite on victims as Count Dracula.

Gerald McRaney: TV's *Major Dad*.

Maigret: Fictional French detective (first name: Jules) created by Georges Simenon. Second only to Sherlock Holmes in puffing his way to solutions to crimes. He chose from a collection of fifteen, kept in his office.

Henry Mancini: One of his songs says it all: "Moon River."

Somerset Maugham: Also an archetypal author–pipe smoker.

Herman Melville: Had a whale of a time whenever he lit up.

Arthur Miller: Archetype of playwright as pipe smoker.

Christopher Morley: Ace Sherlockian, mastermind behind the founding of the New York Holmesian group, The Baker Street Irregulars.

Nick Nolte: Rugged movie actor, rarely without a pipe in the 1997 thriller *U-Turn.*

Pat O'Brien: Actor and quintessential movie Irishman.

Pat O'Brien: The sportscaster.

General George S. Patton: World War II tank commander known as "Old Blood and Guts."

Joseph Peretti: Third-generation Boston tobacconist and pipe maker puffs contentedly as he turns out exquisite products in the workshop at the front of his store in Park Square, opposite historic Boston Commons.

General John J. Pershing: World War I commander of U.S. forces introduced **General MacArthur** to the meerschaums of Missouri (Black Jack's home state).

Walter Pidgeon: Whether he was Greer Garson's husband in *Mrs. Miniver,* the liberal Welsh pastor in *How Green Was My Valley,* or majority leader of the U.S. Senate in *Advise and Consent,* his characterization would have seemed incomplete without a briar in his hand.

Admiral John Poindexter: Kept his pipe going even though he took the fall in the Iran-Contra scandal.

Cole Porter: Sophisticated songwriter of the 1920s and 1930s smoked a straight-stemmed pipe night and day.

William Powell: Defined onscreen male sophistication as Nick Charles in the *Thin Man* series.

Melvin Purvis: FBI agent during the 1930s who tracked down America's public enemies. He smoked a cigar to celebrate the killing of Pretty Boy Floyd by his G-men, and he lit a cigar to signal the feds

to close in for the capture of John Dillinger, who also wound up
dead at Purvis's feet. But when he retired from the FBI (some say
he was forced out by J. Edgar Hoover, who did not like Purvis getting more publicity than himself), Melvin told reporters his immediate retirement goal was to "get a pipe that will hold a pound of
tobacco" then find a rocking chair and rock and smoke very slowly.

James Reston: After him, reporting and interpreting the events of
Washington, D.C., in the *New York Times* would never be the same.

Edward G. Robinson: He had a cigar in his mouth to portray gang-
sters in the movies, but this erudite collector of great art was also a
passionate pipe smoker; the only nonroyal person to have both cigar
and pipe tobaccos named after him.

Norman Rockwell: Painter-illustrator whose *Saturday Evening Post*
covers in the 1940s and 1950s defined the American way of life.
Occasionally he would put himself in the picture, puffing on a briar
or corncob.

Will Rogers: Cowboy humorist of the 1930s never met a pipe or pipe
smoker he didn't like.

Sax Rohmer: Creator of master criminal Dr. Fu Manchu.

Leo Rosten: Author and collector of American humor, mostly of the
Yiddish variety.

George Herman "Babe" Ruth: Baseball's Sultan of Swat.

Anwar Sadat: As president of Egypt, he shattered the anti-Israel soli-
darity of the Arab world in the Camp David accords of 1979, prov-
ing once again that pipe smokers are at heart peaceable people.

Jonas Salk: Inventor of an antipolio vaccine.

Carl Sandburg: Poet, peerless biographer of Abraham Lincoln, and champion of the virtues of Chicago.

George Sanders: Not even smoking a pipe could soften this suave British actor's image as a cad in many movies—a role he admitted playing in real life as well.

Jean-Paul Sartre: I told you pipe smokers were philosophers.

Antonin Scalia: Associate justice, U.S. Supreme Court.

Arthur M. Schlesinger Jr.: Historian. The only things more constant in his life are bow ties and the Kennedys.

James Schlesinger: When he was secretary of defense there was no banning of smoking in the Pentagon.

Charles Schultz: Creator of the comic strip "Peanuts."

Albert Schweitzer: Humanitarian, organist, scientist.

William L. Shirer: Observer and chronicler of the rise and fall of Nazi Germany, he embodied the glamour and daring of the war correspondent in print and on the radio.

Jacques Tati: Mexican-born comedian, best known as valet to **David Niven** in *Around the World in Eighty Days.*

Alfred, Lord Tennyson: Whenever he was at loss for a clever couplet he put aside his quill pen for a smoke break.

Spencer Tracy: He would have been moviedom's greatest actor even if he hadn't smoked pipes.

Pierre Trudeau: Former prime minister of Canada.

Rudolph Valentino: Superstar of silent movies, usually seen offscreen smoking straight-stemmed briars.

Lee Van Cleef: The steely-eyed gunslinger usually puffed a cheroot in western movies but preferred a meer-schaum when not in character.

Vincent van Gogh: Some of the artist's master-pieces included pipes: "Still Life with Straw Hat," "Chair and Pipe," "Still Life with Onions," and a self-portrait with a clay.

When silent film heartthrob Rudolph Valentino was not smoldering on screen he was likely to be found relaxing with a book and a pipe. New York Public Library

Bob Vila: TV fixer-upper, around any house, old or new.

Evelyn Waugh: British author. The PBS-TV series based on his *Brideshead Revisited* was seen by more people than had read the book.

Orson Welles: Frequently photographed in his latter years with a big black cigar matching the dimensions of his enormous body, but a pipe was the choice of the slim and dapper film auteur who made *Citizen Kane* two years after hoodwinking the American people into believing that a Halloween radio dramatization of H. G. Wells's *War of the Worlds* was an actual invasion of Earth by lots of slimy, bug-eyed Martians.

P. G. Wodehouse: His pipe was as indispensable when writing his ninety-two novels as was Jeeves, the gentleman's gentleman in a series of books, to his boss when Bertie Wooster found himself in dire straits, or, as Jeeves put it, "knee-deep in the bisque."

Robert Young: A lifetime of acting in movies did not bring this devoted pipe smoker as much fame and fortune as his role as Dr. Welby on TV in the years when doctors made house calls and the first words out of their mouths were not "Is this visit covered by your health plan?" followed by the mantra, "Stop smoking."

Presidential Pipers

John Adams: Successor to George Washington had smoked clay pipes as a leader of the Revolution and signer of the Declaration of Independence, then continued smoking as the first occupant of the executive mansion in the new capital city named after his predecessor. In a letter to his wife, Abigail, he expressed the hope that none but wise men would preside within its walls. Unfortunately, some of those who followed him didn't live up to that ideal.

Andrew Jackson: When the seventh president first came out of the woods of Tennessee as a congressman he was already the owner of plenty of well-smoked clays and corncobs.

William Henry Harrison: Died one month after taking office as the ninth president (from pneumonia, not because of his pipe smoking).

Ulysses S. Grant: Although the Civil War hero was better known as a cigar man, he'd smoked pipes throughout his dogged pursuit of Rebel troops from Fort Donaldson, where he got the nickname

"Unconditional Surrender," to Robert E. Lee's acceptance of that demand on behalf of the Confederacy in 1865.

Herbert Hoover: Notwithstanding the historic disapproval of pipe smoking by the Quaker church to which the thirty-first President of the White House belonged.

Franklin D. Roosevelt: Before he took up the cigarettes that he smoked through a long-stemmed holder.

Dwight D. Eisenhower: Chiefly a cigarette man, he smoked a pipe at times during his army career, but did not light up any tobacco during his two terms in the presidency.

Richard M. Nixon: He fit the image of pipe smokers as smart, but in the minds of many Americans he was decidedly impeachable in the all-around-nice-guy category.

Gerald R. Ford: Some detractors joked that President Ford's pipe smoking was the exception that proved the rule that all pipe smokers are extremely intelligent. But he revalidated the image of President-as-nice-guy.

Ronald Reagan: A pre–White House pipe smoker.

George Bush: On his long road from Yale to White House.

Bill Clinton: Even if he wanted to light a pipe he wouldn't dare, because Hillary banned smoking anywhere in the White House.

The World's Most Famous Pipe Smoker

Except perhaps for watches and bootlaces, Sherlock Holmes explained to Dr. Watson in *The Hound of the Baskervilles,* "nothing has more individuality than a pipe."

Although many Sherlockians believe that the calabash pipe was made a part of the Sherlock Holmes silhouette by the actor William Gillette, recent scholarship indicates that the bulky pipe was first put into Holmes's hand by a comedian in a non-Sherlockian movie titled The Nitwits.
New York Public Library

Certainly there has been no individual, real or fictional, more associated with pipe smoking than the resident of London's 221B Baker Street who claimed to be the world's first private consulting detective and the author of a monograph, "Upon the Distinction between the Ashes of the Various Tobaccos."

Observation of tobacco ash proved to be decisive in the solution of several Holmesian cases, and pipes appear in all but four of the sixty Sherlockian adventures penned by Sir Arthur Conan Doyle.

Although Holmes smoked cigars (he kept them in a coal scuttle) and cigarettes, the pipe was unquestionably his preference, especially when pondering the intricacies of whatever "problem" presented itself.

In an analysis of his smoking habits titled "140 Different Varieties," British Sherlockian expert John Hall surmised that the sedative properties of Holmes's strong shag tobacco "may have helped relax the detective's mind so that he was able to concentrate more effectively."

He is depicted smoking a pipe in thirty-five cases, and there are references to the many pipes he owned (Dr. Watson noted "a litter of pipes" on the mantelpiece), from briars to the previously mentioned cherrywood, and an old clay that was black and oily. Another (type not specified) was deemed by Dr. Watson to be "unsavory."

Illustrators of the Holmes stories that appeared in *Strand* magazine in England and in reprints in American magazines put a briar in his hand, usually one with a straight stem. It was not until Holmes became a character in movies that there appeared the bent pipe stem that has become as indelibly a part of Holmes's image as the Inverness and deerstalker.

While it was the bent briar (a Peterson) that Basil Rathbone smoked in his fourteen films as Sherlock, Granada Television's definitive portrayer of the sleuth of Baker Street, Jeremy Brett, smoked a variety of pipes, including an impressive churchwarden.

Yet it's the calabash that has become the enduring symbol of Holmes as pipe smoker, despite the fact that there is no mention of a calabash in any of Conan Doyle's stories. Tradition has it that the pipe was an innovation of William Gillette for his 1901 play *Sherlock Holmes* and that Conan Doyle granted permission for the use of a meerschaum-lined calabash.

However, in "The Great Calabash Question" in the June 1997 edition of the *Baker Street Journal* ("An Irregular Quarterly of Sherlockiana" published under the auspices of the Baker Street Irregulars of New York), Robert S. Ennis traced the origin of the Sherlockian calabash to Robert Woolsey of the vaudeville team Wheeler and Woolsey in a 1935 film, *The Nitwits*. Its next appearance on film was in comedian Lou Costello's hand in a Holmesian burlesque, *Abbott and Costello Meet the Invisible Man* (1951).

"What is almost certain," John Hall deduced in "140 Different Varieties, "is that Holmes is very unlikely to have been much of an enthusiast for the calabash, even if he did own one. The gourd acts as an expansion chamber, not only cooling the smoke—acceptable enough—but also removing some of the tars and nicotine from it, and that is not likely to find much favour with a man who habitually smokes the strongest tobacco he can buy."

The tobacco was shag.

But what about Watson? Which tobacco did he prefer? When getting acquainted with his roommate he spoke of smoking a type known as "ship's," which was a very cheap and exceedingly powerful kind of twisted plug. But later Holmes observed that Watson was "still smoking that Arcadia mixture of your bachelor days."

Noting that Holmes mentioned the "bachelor days" of the doctor, it is elementary that Watson had gotten married. That he was still a smoker proved his bride was an exceptional person.

Pipes and Women

With a few exceptions, smoking a pipe has always been a masculine thing. But, as every male knows, nothing a man does goes unnoticed by the women in his life, and nothing that a man may wish to do proceeds without feminine acquiescence if the relationship is to last. History teaches that in this delicate equation only the male's pursuit of "the other woman" and excessive drinking have outranked smoking in the disdain of the majority of women. It is historical fact that, by and large, women have not been big fans of tobacco.

In the earliest days of tobacco smoking in England (1605), a character in George Chapman's poetic play *All Fools* said to his friends, no doubt driven by experience with women who objected to smoking:

> *And for discourse in my fair mistress's presence*
> *I did not, as you barren gallants do,*
> *Fill my discourses up drinking tobacco.*

Eight years later in a burlesque comedy, *The Knight of the Burning Pestle,* by Beaumont and Fletcher, a woman declared to a group of such gallants, "Now I pray, gentlemen, what good does this stinking tobacco do you? Nothing, I warrant you, but make chimneys of your faces."

In Thackeray's satirical "Fitz-Boodle Papers," published in *Frasier's Magazine* in 1842, the main character confessed, "I am not, in the first place, what is called a ladies' man, having contracted an irrepressible habit of smoking after dinner, which has obliged me to give up a great deal of the dear creatures' society."

Venturing a guess as to why women objected to smoking, Fitz-Boodle continued, "I believe in my heart that women are jealous of it, as of a rival. They speak of it as of some secret awful vice that seizes upon a man and makes him a pariah from genteel society."

The dilemma for smokers in the face of this feminine antismoking attitude also found voice in a poem by Rudyard Kipling in which a man was forced by the woman he hoped to marry to make a choice between giving her up and abandoning his cigars. Weighing the pros and cons of each, the poem concluded with the best-known quotation in the lore of tobacco: "A woman is just a woman, but a good cigar is a smoke."

Because Kipling also smoked a pipe, the line could just as readily have substituted "pipe" for "cigar."

Although smokers of Kipling's time found themselves unwelcome in the palaces of antitobacco Queen Victoria, Her Majesty found herself in a diplomatic quandary as a result of an exchange of gifts between herself and the King of Dahomey. As a token of Britain's esteem, she had sent the Eastern monarch a damask tent, a silver pipe, and a pair of silver trays. Unfortunately, as the king reported to the bearer of the gifts, Sir Richard Burton, the tent was too small, the trays hardly large enough to be used as shields, and the pipe smoked poorly. The king's hopes had been that Victoria would send him a carriage and a pair of horses to draw it, along with a white woman. Despite his disappointment, he sent Victoria by way of Burton a fine West African umbrella, some colorful fabrics, and several native pipes that he prayed Her Britannic Majesty would enjoy.

When Victoria's reign, which had begun in 1837, ended in 1901, the men of her court greeted with delight an announcement from Victoria's long-suffering cigar-smoking son, the Prince of Wales. As he became Edward VII, he declared, "Gentlemen, you may smoke."

But the king's permission applied only to royal real estate. What went on in a man's home was entirely up to "the woman of the house." Rare was the male smoker anywhere who was not warned by a wife against dropping his ashes on the carpet, or who had not had to listen to a mate's complaints that "everything in the house smells" of tobacco.

In 1878 a sort of Victorian guide to acceptable intergender behavior *(Mr. Punch's Pocket-Book)* cited a wife's ideal husband as a nonsmoker, while a man's ideal wife would let him "smoke all over the house."

Yet the same publication's article titled "Cupid and Baccy" went on to present a conversation between a youth and his uncle that brought out a surprising fact about the view of some Victorian women toward pipe smoking.

"No fellow can fall in love when he has continually a pipe in his mouth," warned the stodgy uncle. Pointing out that "in my time" smoking in the presence of a lady was "an inconceivable outrage," he demanded, "Why do you do it?"

The youth retorted, "The girls like it."

And more than a century later, even in face of increasing intolerance of tobacco by health extremists—who evidently believe that anything they don't like, including mortality, can be legislated out of existence—there appears to be room for an exemption for the pipe. While revulsion among women to the smell of cigarettes and cigars (especially cigars!) seems to be a universal and persistent phenomenon, protests against the aroma of burning pipe tobacco by women reach nothing near the intensity of the griping about cigarettes and cigars. Rather than being fixed with a withering glare of condemnation, a man smoking a pipe near a woman is likely to hear, "I like your tobacco."

This could well be a manifestation of the findings of the Criswell survey discussed in chapter 3, in which 90 percent of women across all age groups expressed the opinion that a man who smokes a pipe is *sexy*.

In interpreting the Criswell statistics in *The Pipe Smoker,* authors John Paul Beaumier and Lewis Camp concluded, "What women see is the patient and skillful manner in which [a pipe smoker] creates his own sensual enjoyment: the gentleness, the slowness, the attentiveness, the unfeigned delight, the immersion of all the senses in a ritualistic revel that is almost trancelike."

While the Criswell survey took the scientific approach to the mystique of the pipe, numerous writers have resorted to poetry to make the connection between pipe smoking and the male-female relationship. In "An Old Sweetheart of Mine" the esteemed author James Whitcomb Riley wrote:

> *A face of lily beauty, with a form of airy grace,*
> *Floats out of my tobacco as the "Genii" from the vase;*
> *And I thrill beneath the glances of a pair of azure eyes,*
> *As glowing as the summer and as tender as the skies.*

Pipe-Smoking Women

While the overwhelming majority of women have gone on record against smoking of all kinds, the pages of history are not without a few who not only did not object to their men smoking pipes, but also defied convention and took up pipes themselves.

One who did so in 1700 was a friend of the English writer Thomas Brown, who wrote to her, "Though the ill-natured World *censures* you for Smoaking, yet I would advice you, Madam, not to part with so innocent a Diversion. . . . It is heathful . . . is a great help to

Christian Meditations . . . [and] is a pretty plaything . . . [that] is fashionable [and] a fair way of becoming so."

Following the introduction of tobacco to Europe when women were as eager to try smoking as men, colonists carried pipes back to the continent where tobacco had originated. As rudimentary settlements thrived and grew into villages, then towns, and at last cities, women who had smoked pipes in the lands of the Old World continued to do so in colonial America. One of these was Sarah Fell. Step-daughter of the Quaker preacher George Fox, she noted in her diary that she had purchased tobacco and clay pipes for her sister Susannah.

In all likelihood these young women did not smoke in public, or often. While Quakers did not object to smoking, they frowned upon using tobacco frequently. Minutes of the Friend's Monthly Meeting at Hardshaw, Lancashire, England, noted the common view that "it is desired that such as have occasion to make use thereof take it privately, neither too publicly in their own houses, nor by the highways, streets, or in alehouses or elsewhere."

In 1756 a group of Quakers returning to England for a visit sailed down the Delaware River from William Penn's Philadelphia aboard a ship named *The Charming Polly*. A diarist

Beginning with the introduction of tobacco to England, pipe smoking proved lastingly popular with many women, including 96-year-old Martha Barnes in this watercolor painting by Lucius Barnes, c. 1834.
New York Public Library

noted that in passenger Samuel Fothergill's "new chest" were "Tobacco . . . a Hamper . . . a Barrel . . . a box of pipes." Other passengers included Mary Peisly and Katherine Payton. In their sea chests were balm, sage, summer savory, horehound, oranges, two bottles of brandy and two of "Jamaica Spirrit," a canister of green tea, a jar of almond paste, gingerbread, tobacco, and a box of pipes.

Certainly, the British Isles to which they journeyed were by then accustomed to women smoking pipes.

One English woman whose obituary appeared in a newspaper in 1856 was a widow, Jane Garbett. According to the *Darlington and Stockton Times*, she went to her deathbed at the age of 110 "free from pain, retaining all her faculties to the last, and enjoying her pipe."

A reporter who had visited her the year before noted that as a "brother-piper" he had taken her tobacco as a gift. Asked how long she'd smoked, Jane answered, "Very nearly a hundred years."

Another case of a venerable pipe smoker, cited in Apperson's *The Social History of Smoking,* was a woman named Pheasy Molly, who died at ninety-six. Her demise was attributed to the accidental ignition of her clothes as she was lighting her pipe at the fire. "She had burned herself more than once before in performing the same operation," Apperson noted, "but her pipe she was bound to have, and so met her end."

Both these accounts attest to the fact that pipe smoking by women was once a common sight in Europe and in America. Anyone who has seen the movie version of Charles Dickens's epic of the French Revolution, *A Tale of Two Cities,* starring Ronald Colman, will recall Madame Defarge seated outside a shop puffing a long clay pipe as she knitted into a blanket the names of people whom she deemed worthy of going to the guillotine.

A nineteenth-century poem described a woman selling apples on a street:

> *Betty Bouncer kept a stall*
> *At the corner of a street,*
> *And she had a smile for all.*
> *Many were the friends she'd greet*
> *With kindly nod on passing by,*
> *Who, smiling, saw her pipe awry.*

Also in the nineteenth century lived a Baroness Duvant, whose given name was Amandine Aurore Lucie Dupin. Better known in literature by the masculine nom de plume George Sand, she favored a carved cherrywood. In the 1920s Gertrude Stein smoked a pipe while presiding over literary salons in her Parisian apartment attended by Ernest Hemingway and other writers, and avant-garde artists such as Pablo Picasso.

The only American first lady to smoke pipes in the White House was Mrs. Zachary Taylor, but she had to smuggle them into the executive mansion and enjoy them behind closed doors.

A political woman who smoked pipes openly from the 1960s through the 1980s was New Jersey's Republican congresswoman Millicent Fenwick. She had been advised by a doctor to give up cigarettes and switched to a briar pipe and smaller varieties, which were often brilliantly colored. Her public displays of pipe smoking triggered a failed attempt by pipe makers to market a wide variety of decorated diminutive pipes to women. The campaign did not catch on, chiefly because women smokers preferred cigarettes.

Other prominent women of the past who eschewed them and the cigar and dared convention by smoking pipes in public included

Madame Pompadour and the painters Élisabeth Vigée-Lebrun and Rosa Bonheur.

And there was Lupe Velez. A 1940s stage and movie actress with a reputation as a "Latin bombshell," she exhibited no fear of damaging her career in allowing herself to be revealed as a pipe smoker in a three-page article, "Lupe Lights Up," in the movie fan magazine *Pic*.

10

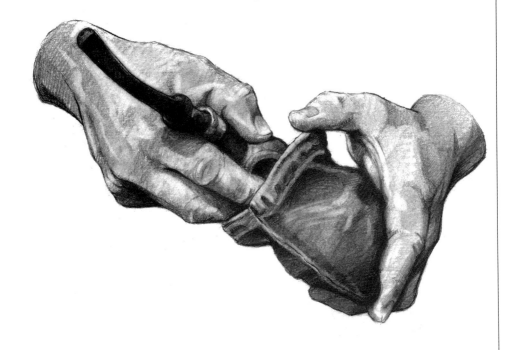

Pipe Dreams

*"Here's the $64 question—are old pipe tins really
worth what people ask for them?"*

—LETTER FROM A SUBSCRIBER TO *THE PIPE
SMOKER'S EPHEMERIS*

*H*alf a century after Lupe Velez was a movie star, only the most dedicated students of old films are likely to recall her. But she captured the affection of pipe smokers in the form of a 1997 edition of *The Pipe Smoker's Ephemeris* when it reproduced the cover of the old fan magazine showing her zestfully smoking a long-stemmed briar.

Defined by founder-publisher-editor Tom Dunn as "an irregular quarterly for pipe smokers," the *Ephemeris* brims on every page with data, opinions of readers, and advice and guidance on all aspects of pipe smoking. It is the journal of "The Universal Coterie of Pipe Smokers," one of many groups established in the United States and around the world committed to ensuring that the candle lit four centuries ago by Raleigh will never flicker out.

If Sir Walter were to somehow manage to come back to life at the close of the twentieth century, he would dis-

The Pipe Smoker's Ephemeris, founded in 1964 by editor and publisher Tom Dunn, is "a limited-edition, irregular quarterly for pipe smokers and anyone else interested in its varied contents." The front page of the Spring-Summer 1997 volume had a picture of pipe-smoking 1940s movie star Lupe Velez.
Tom Dunn

cover that pipe smoking is not experiencing a decline, but rebounding. It is a growth in popularity that may be attributed in part to a surge in the popularity of cigars that began in the early 1990s. This sudden adoption of cigars and the springing up of cigar bars, clubs, and "cigar evenings" was described by sociologists as a manifestation of a burgeoning rebellion against both the smoke police and a feminist movement that many men viewed as ultrastrident and outright antimale.

One result of the dramatic increase in cigar smoking has been an uptick in pipe smoking. According to a 1997 survey by the magazine *Tobacconist,* the tobacco industry anticipated a jump of 19.2 percent in pipe sales over the next two years. To Dayton Matlick of *Pipes and Tobaccos* magazine this rise in pipe smoking appeared to be a result of smokers seeking an alternative to quitting smoking. He told *USA Today,* "People are looking for opportunities to smoke less but to enjoy it more."

Pipes also presented an economical alternative to rapidly rising costs of premium cigars in response to increased demand. Detecting some deflation in the boom in stogies, the co-owner of New York's Beekman Bar and Books, Mark Grossich, told a reporter that "cigars have played out a bit," and "the time is ripe to reintroduce the joys of pipe smoking."

To do this, Grossich started holding pipe-smoking events similar to those that had helped launch the cigar comeback.

The rekindling of interest in pipe smoking was also demonstrated in the form of two magazines—*Smoke* and *Pipes and Tobaccos.* Although the former made its debut and rode to success on the cigar tide, the lively quarterly has also picked up on the revival in pipe smoking by introducing a separate section devoted to pipes and pipe tobaccos. The latter is even newer than *Smoke,* but it devotes all its pages to pipes and pipe tobaccos, if not quite as breezily or entertainingly as *Smoke.*

European publications devoted to pipes are found in Belgium, Denmark, England, France, Germany, Ireland, and the Netherlands.

The Internet

By any standard in the 1990s, a reliable barometer of the popular trends of the waning years of the second millennium was the rapid expansion of worldwide instant communication through the personal computer known as the Internet. A cursory scan of the offerings of the America Online service one summer evening afforded a browser more than eighty links to commercial pipe-related enterprises, ranging from the Barcelona Pipa Club to Yahoo's Pipe Pointers. "Personal Pipe Links" began with "Alan Peschke's Pictures of People with Pipes" and ended with "Kaywoodie Collectors Page." Pipe organizations run the alphabet, from the Assen Pipe Smoking Guild to the Triad Tampers of Greensboro, High Point and Winston-Salem, North Carolina. And there were AOL sites on such varied topics as the proper way to puff, articles from *Pipes Digest,* and an old advertisement for Dr. Grabow pipes explaining the correct way to smoke pipes.

The Organization of Online Pipe Smokers (OoOPS) is one of a growing number of sources of information on pipes and smoking available to users of the Internet.

On the World Wide Web the Organization of Online Pipe Smokers (OoOPS) offered information on pipe smoking and collecting, and invited cyberspacers to join the club and receive its monthly newsletter, *Blowing Smoke.*

The OoOPS Website offered noncommercial material on a wide range of topics and commercial offerings, from pipe maker Alberto Bonfigliol to the Georgetown Tobacco chain of stores in the Washington, D.C., area; Kirsten Pipes; Marty Pulver's Sherlock's Haven store in San Francisco; Paykoc Imports, Inc., on the subject of meerschaums; and Olde World Fine Clays.

Because of the proliferation (and disappearance) of Websites devoted to pipes in particular and smoking in general, the surest way to locate them is to browse.

Pipes in the News

Newspapers and magazines have also detected the trend toward pipes. Among the articles published in 1997 were "Pipe Smoking Gains Fans with Hip and Trendy, Young and Old" *(Detroit News);* "More U.S. Smokers Ponder Merits of the Bowl and Stem" (*Chicago Tribune,* January 6, 1997); and "Like Their Cousins Cigars, Pipes Are Hot Again" by the same paper on December 14, 1996.

That same week *USA Today's* "The Good Life" page carried an article by Cathy Hainer under the banner headline A REKINDLED PASSION FOR PIPE SMOKING TAKES HOLD.

She began, "They're coming out of tweedy men's clubs and heading into the hottest nightspots." In addition to reporting on the upsurge in pipe smoking, Hainer went on to offer a condensed primer on the subject that contrasted pipes and cigars and their tobaccos. Accompanying sidebars included advice on how to find the right pipe and "accessories for lighting up, from pouches to humidors."

Fortune magazine also joined a growing list of publications looking at all aspects of pipes and pipe smoking with an article titled "Pipe Dreams." The subtitle ("Refurbished Estate Pipes Are Collectible, Tasty—and Refreshingly Unhip") served to introduce an activity—some would term it an obsession—whose existence probably surprised many of the magazine's readers.

Pipe Collecting

This is a subject about which you might feel compelled to repeat Juliet's lament to Romeo, "What's in a name?"

In pipe collecting famous names can be as significant to collectors as Tiffany is to lamps; Paul Revere to silver; Shaker, Chippendale, Mies van der Rohe, and Jules Leleu to furniture; and Mark Twain, Hemingway, and Steinbeck to collectors of literary first editions.

There is not a pipe collector who would not agree—to paraphrase A. S. W. Rosenbach in *A Book Hunter's Holiday*—that after love, pipe collecting is the most exhilarating sport of all.

In the 1969 edition of Alfred Dunhill's *The Pipe Book,* a comprehensive history of pipes and pipe making around the world, the list of illustrations of pipes requires six and a half pages. The 260 pipes that are pictured range from an ancient one made of twisted leaf of the sal tree to an exquisitely carved meerschaum in the form of an old man with a bushy curled beard and wearing a night cap with a long tassel. All of the pipes shown in the book are part of the Dunhill pipe collection.

That a giant of pipe manufacturing, and a historian of pipes as well, would have been a collector should hardly come as a revelation. Nor is it a cause for raised eyebrows to note that wealthy men who smoked pipes might desire to accumulate them in large quantities.

It is unremarkable, therefore, to point out that pipe collections were built by puffing members of European aristocracy, Egypt's infamously rich King Farouk, and the elite of Hollywood, past and present. It's one of the charms that oodles of money and a superior credit rating confer on those who've been bitten by the urge to obtain pleasure by accumulating as many rare objects of a kind as they can merely for the fun of doing so.

But what about Mr. Average Pipe Smoker? What is there that would motivate a man of modest means to become a collector?

The answer to this question may be found in a poem called "The Collector" in a volume titled *The Light Guitar* (1923) by Arthur Guilerman:

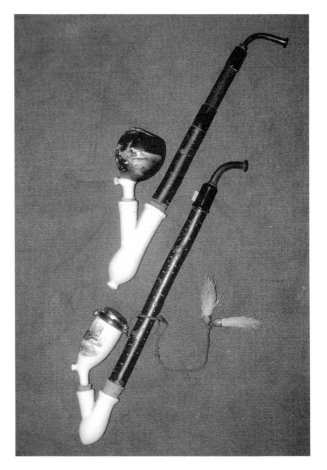

Artistry and materials make these porcelain pipes highly collectible.
© Kevin Gordon

> *Beware the Gimlet-eyed Collector*
> *Who haunts the manse,—a Ghoul, a Specter!—*
> *That, when Aged Owner dies,*
> *He may achieve some Battered Prize!*

What makes an object prized? Ask any collector and you'll be told it is beauty, workmanship, quality, age, and rarity. But most especially rarity: to own what is no longer available and to possess, one hopes, what no one else has or may obtain.

If these criteria apply to antique furniture, books, paintings, porcelain teapots and dinner plates, silverware, teddy bears, baseball trading cards, and practically everything else under the sun, why shouldn't they extend to pipes?

WHAT MAKES A PIPE COLLECTIBLE?

As in all kinds of collecting, there are five reasons for acquiring a pipe: because you love it for itself, because it's in reasonably good condition, for its rarity, for the quality and workmanship of the maker, and because of the price being demanded.

The first of these criteria is the most important. It makes as little sense to buy a pipe that doesn't immediately win your heart as it does to enter into a loveless marriage; the result can be just as frustrating.

Unless you have stumbled upon a pipe with such overriding historical significance that it belongs in a museum, neither is there any logic in collecting a pipe in such bad condition that it is hopelessly beyond reviving. (Restoring pipes is discussed below.)

Rarity and uniqueness are always good reasons to buy something, as are quality and workmanship as indicated by the name of the maker—but not at the expense of the first two and the last of the above criteria. Why own a rare, unique, famous-name pipe if it is in lousy shape and utterly unlovable, especially if you can't really afford it?

But there is a further aspect of pipe collecting that does not apply to most kinds of collectibles, which wind up being put on display or locked away for safekeeping. Like collectors of antique or unique automobiles, boats, bicycles, and airplanes, most pipe collectors acquire a vintage pipe in order to use it.

This frequently requires restoring its smokability.

RESTORING PIPES

Most pipes that find their way into the hands of collectors need only a little sprucing up on the outside and cleaning of the bowl, shank, and stem. Materials to accomplish these tasks may be obtained from a tobacconist. If stems need to be replaced or a shank or bowl has to be repaired, there are firms that specialize in these tasks. (See "Sources" at the back of this book.)

If it's a very old pipe worthy of being classified as an antique, the wise thing to do is turn it over to a professional restorer or an expert at a museum.

COLLECTIBLE BRANDS

Virtually every pipe carrying the name of the esteemed manufacturers discussed in chapter 5 has been deemed collectible. Among those sought most by American collectors are Barling, Charatan, and Sasieni, as well as the two most widely recognized of the major names: Peterson and Dunhill.

Peterson pipes are classified by shapes that are described either by numbers or by names such as Tankard, Belgique, and Barrel. The company offers brochures that serve as guides for collectors.

Dunhill, regarded as the most collectible brand, has been the company most meticulous in dating pipes by way of a stamped numerical code signifying the year of manufacture. In the 1970s there were two digits, starting with 11, which stood for 1971. A 12 denoted 1972, and so on. In the 1980s the first digit was a 2, so that 22 meant the pipe had been made in 1982.

Prior to 1955, a Dunhill carried its patent number and a single digit for the patent year. The firm also distinguished its bowl sizes and shapes by a system of letters, though this practice was discontinued in 1975.

If all this seems confusing to you, the feeling is not yours alone. A column by Richard Esserman in the Spring-Summer 1997 *Pipe Smoker's Ephemeris* lamented "a paucity of information concerning pre-1925 Dunhill information." He continued, "There are esoteric issues, [such] as which is older, a Bruyere stamped with A (without a circle) or an A with circle?"

Esoteric issues, indeed!

But for one American-made pipe that is regarded by many collectors as highly desirable there can be no confusion regarding dates of manufacture.

Kaywoodie shapes listed by number in a company-provided list filling four and a half pages of single-spaced typing paper. Beginning with a 1935 Dublin short stem (shape number 00A) and ending with a 1961–1967 model H9 "Hi-Bowl Series," the list totals 430. Names number ninety. And there are nine matched-grain and collector's presentation sets priced from fifty to thirty-five hundred dollars.

The best way to start collecting pipes is to read as much as you can. Manufacturers and tobacconists are prime sources for information. Two excellent books also provide guidance: Hacker's *The Ultimate Pipe Book* (chapter 9) and *A Complete Guide to Collecting Antique Pipes,* by Benjamin Rapaport (1979).

Collecting Tobacco Tins

Although the author of this book is not a pipe collector, only a smoker, a "battered prize" that will leave his possession only after his death is a part of his collection of Sherlockiana. It's an empty round tobacco tin. Made by FDB Cigar-OG Tobaksfabrikker of Denmark and called "a carefully balanced blend" of medium-strength tobaccos, it was named "No. 221 B Baker Street Mixture."

The lid of the tin is white with black printing, except for the *221,* which is red. A reproduction in black and white of what appears to be an old etching shows a hansom cab waiting next to a gas street-lamp in front of what may be deduced is the most famous address in crime fiction. The cabbie appears to be waiting in expectation of hearing the cry "The game's afoot," followed by the appearance of Sherlock Holmes. If so, the driver is wasting his time, for it was Sherlock's inviolate rule of personal safety never to hail the first cab in line—where an enemy who did not know Holmes's habits might be lurking—but only the third.

Whether my 221 B tin is valuable, I have no idea; nor do I care. As a doomed-to-be-murdered collector of musical boxes said in a Rathbone Holmes movie *(Dressed to Kill),* "A collector buys, but never sells." My 221 B tin, along with the rest of my Holmes collection (including a Sherlock Holmes cigar box), is in my will for fellow Sherlockian Kevin Gordon, whose drawings grace this book.

Should I—or you—decide to plunge into a hobby that is as daunting and complex as tobacco-tin collecting, the first step, as in pipe collecting, is to study the subject.

Tobacco appeared in tins in the 1890s, around the same time as biscuits and other foods. In addition to better maintaining the freshness of the contents, the switch from paper to metal packaging helped foster brand identity and loyalty, because advances in the technology of printing, especially in color, made it possible for the name of the maker to be fixed to the tin as a glued-on label, or printed directly on the metal.

Brand names quickly proliferated and soon ran the gamut from outdoor motifs (Stag, Tiger, Rod and Reel) to historical personalities (George Washington, Abraham Lincoln, John Paul Jones, and, of course, Sir Walter Raleigh and Prince Albert). With the popularization of baseball, stars of the diamond found their way onto tins. At

Tobacco tins were introduced in the 1890s. Although they were made by the billions, few survived, thereby giving rise to a brisk collectors market. No doubt, some of these modern brands will be deemed "treasures" a century from now.
© Kevin Gordon

the close of the nineteenth century a catalog of tobacco brands being sold in the United States, Britain, and Canada listed more than two thousand names. Four decades later the tonnage of sheet steel used for tobacco containers surpassed forty thousand, enough to hold ninety thousand tons of tobacco in a billion tins.

Yet the ones that escaped being tossed away amount to a very few, comparatively. That is why a tobacco-tin collector must be prepared to pay. You don't have to be a Sherlock Holmes to deduce that their very scarcity is why they are collectible.

A letter in the Autumn 1996 edition of *The Pipe Smoker's Ephemeris* from the incipient collector whose query appears at the beginning of this chapter illustrates the point:

> I found lots of Prince Albert, Velvet, and Half and Half tins, the small rectangular kind, [but] the cheapest one . . . was $8. It didn't look like much . . . the paint was chipped, and there were a couple of dents in it. Prices went up from there. I found a couple of the larger, round cans . . . but they were at least $20.

The writer continued, "Are these things really that rare? Or is this a case of people being silly enough to pay big bucks for a run-of-the-mill tin? Am I missing something?"

Ephemeris editor Tom Dunn replied, "It's the educated consumer who will *not* get burned. Save your money for that special, fine condition tin that turns you on."

Sound counsel! But where does a person who wants to collect pipe-tobacco tins learn? One way is to subscribe to Tom Dunn's publication (see "Sources") and check the pages in it that deal with tin collecting, including listings of the dealers in such items, and of others who offer catalogs in the field of pipes and tobaccos. The publication also carries notices sent in by experienced collectors seeking the varieties of tins that are their special interest. These appeals can inform and educate.

One of the regular contributors to the *Ephemeris,* Richard Esserman, collects Dunhill tins. The various mixtures are denoted by numbers, making it fairly easy to recognize any gaps in the collection. But there are subtler differences that Esserman pointed out, including variances in the script used in the Dunhill name. Most have the name in tall, lower-case, modern-looking letters. But the fancy script on a tin of Mixture 965 has an upper-case *D*. The tin also notes the contents were "manufactured under authority of the trade mark owner," while certain special mixtures sold only from the Dunhill London store bear the stamp HAND BLENDED and carry Dunhill's St. James's, London, address.

Pipe-tobacco-tin collectors also employ a language of their own. Based on the size and shape of the tins, the terms seem self-explanatory. Examples: *large flat pockets, small flat pockets, small top canisters, square-corner boxes, vertical square-corner boxes,* and *small square-corner boxes.* An auction catalog might refer to a Honeymoon VP. Honeymoon is the brand and the VP means "vertical pocket." Tops are defined by the ways they are opened. Flip means the top is hinged (usually a VP). A pry must be pried or twisted off and is generally round and flat, as is my 221 B tin. Some come with a screw top. Others are canisters with a lid that is lifted (called a lift top, obviously) by yanking a knob.

Costs? At a 1997 auction conducted by mail and telephone a Honeymoon VP in reasonably good condition was priced at $90. A near-mint-condition Wagon Wheel VP was $1,036.

Helpful information on collecting tobacco tins and pipes may be obtained by joining a group of pipe enthusiasts.

Pipe Clubs and Shows

There are many across the country. The easiest way to learn of one in your vicinity is to ask your tobacconist.

Also watch out for advertisements and announcements in your local newspaper for pipe shows and exhibitions. Many clubs sponsor these events. One of the biggest is held annually by the New York Pipe Club, although its event on March 8, 1997, was held in Newark, New Jersey.

Another perennial exposition is sponsored, usually in the autumn, by the Conclave of Richmond Pipe Smokers (C.O.R.P.S.) of Richmond, Virginia. One of the show's most popular and entertaining events is a pipe-smoking contest. The purpose is to see who can keep a pipe lit longest. The winner of the 1996 competition went one hour, nineteen minutes, and forty-three seconds, bettering the runner-up by twenty-eight seconds. The third came in at 1:14:05.

One of the oldest pipe-smoking competitions (the forty-ninth was held in May 1997) is held in the region of Flint, Michigan, and is sponsored by a local pipe store (Paul's Pipe Shop) and three pipe clubs: The Arrowhead, Dave's Smokin' Post, and Tri-Cities.

Perhaps the newest pipe club is in Pennsylvania. The Pipe Club of Philadelphia held its first gathering in September 1996.

Many pipe clubs also have publications that contain not only news about members and club activities, but also information on pipes, tobaccos, and, of course, collecting.

Quotations on Pipes and Smoking

Nothing serves life and soundness of body so well, nor is so necessary as the smoke of the royal plant, tobacco.

—DR. CORNELIUS BONTEKOE, 1685

Where there is idleness, weeds thrive; where there is diligence, tobacco flourishes.

    —BULGARIAN PROVERB

Diplomacy is entirely a question of the weed. I can always settle a quarrel if I know before hand whether the plenipotentiary smokes Cavendish, Latakia, or Shag.

    —LORD CLARENDON, BRITISH FOREIGN SECRETARY

Smoke. Smoke. Smoke. Only a pipe distinguishes man from beast.

    —HONORÉ DAUMIER

Pipe: a primary masculine symbol with authoritarian overtones but also indicative of reliability and contentment.

    —Dictionary of Visual Language, 1980

I believe pipe smoking contributes to a somewhat calm and objective judgment in all human affairs.

    —ALBERT EINSTEIN

When all is said and done, love is trite compared with the spirituality of a tobacco pipe.

    —JULES DE GANCOURT

If discord has broken out between two beings, let them smoke together. United by this bond, they will live in peace and friendship thereafter.

    —THE GREAT MANITOU, THE GREAT SPIRIT

The meerschaum is but a poor affair until it has burned a thousand offerings to the cloud-compelling deities.

    —OLIVER WENDELL HOLMES, *The Autocrat of the Breakfast Table*

For my part, I consider that tobacco, in moderation, is a sweetener and equalizer of the temper.

 —THOMAS H. HUXLEY

A pipe is to the troubled soul what caresses of a mother are for her suffering child.

 —INDIAN PROVERB

May my last breath be drawn through a pipe, and exhaled in a jest.

 —CHARLES LAMB

A pipe in the mouth makes it clear that there has been no mistake—you are undoubtedly a man.

 —A.A. MILNE

Tobacco is the passion of honest men and he who lives without tobacco is not worthy of living.

 —MOLIÈRE

Pipe smoking is properly an intellectual exercise.

 —CHRISTOPHER MORLEY

Man, the creature who knows he must die, who has dreams larger than his destiny, who is forever working a confidence trick on himself, needs an ally. Mine has been tobacco.

 —J. B. PRIESTLEY

A man should always be pleasantly conscious of the fact that he is smoking.

 —IBID.

I have some friends, some honest friends, and honest friends are few;
My pipe of briar, my open fire,
A book that's not too new.

—ROBERT SERVICE

I smoke a pipe abroad, because
To all cigars I much prefer it,
And as I scorn your social laws,
My choice has nothing to deter it.

—ROBERT LOUIS STEVENSON

Allah made tobacco grow to put a smile on the faces of men.

—TURKISH PROVERB

If you can't send money, send tobacco.

—GENERAL GEORGE WASHINGTON TO A CASH-POOR
CONTINENTAL CONGRESS, 1776

Blessed be the man who invented smoking, the soother and comforter of a troubled spirit, allayer of angry passions, a comfort under loss of breakfast, and to the roamer of desolate places, the solitary wayfarer through life, serving for wife, children and friends.

—ANONYMOUS

Nowhere in the world will such a brotherly feeling of confidence be experienced as amongst those who sit together smoking their pipes.

—"THE RESULTS AND MERITS OF TOBACCO," 1844

The Lasting Passion for Pipes

If it were possible for Sir Walter Raleigh to reattach his head, rise from his tomb, and wander around London then cross the Atlantic to see what became of the colony he helped to found (but never got to visit), he could only smile at the realization that the candle he lit in the form of his pipe has not been extinguished. Rather, it has brightened the lives of millions of smokers in his own country, across America, and around the world, and continues to do so whenever and wherever a man or occasional woman draws up a chair to settle back for a little of the peace and quiet, comfort, and contentment that a pipe bestows.

And, no doubt, Sir Walter would appreciate what an anonymous poet meant when he wrote:

> *O my brierwood pipe!—of bright fancy the twin,*
> *What a medley of forms you create;*
> *Every puff of white smoke a vision as fair*
> *As the poet's bright dream, and like dreams fade in air,*
> *While the dreamer dreams on his fate.*

And Raleigh might wonder, as did another writer:

> *Why, what is this? The pipe gone out?*
> *   Well, well, the fire's out, too!*
> *The dreams are gone—we're poor once more;*
> *   Life's pain begins anew.*
> *'Tis time for sleep, my faithful pipe,*
> *   But may thy dreamings be,*
> *Through slumbering hours hued as bright*
> *   As those thou gav'st to me!*

It has been and always will be the delight of the smoker that a pipe is a companion and comforter that, once met and befriended, is yours for life. An when the day comes that it's smoked for the final time it can be laid aside with no regrets, in the spirit of yet another verse:

> *We've been together nearly thirty years, old fellow!*
> *And now, you must admit, we're both a trifle mellow.*
> *We have had our share of joys and a deal of sorrows,*
> *And while we're only waiting for a few more tomorrows,*
> *Others will come, and others will go,*
> *And Time will gather what Youth will sow;*
> *But we together will go down the rough*
> *Road to the end, and to the end—puff.*

But poet Richard le Gallienne wondered:

> *When that last pipe is smoked at last*
> *   And pouch and pipe put by,*
> *And Smoked and Smoker both alike*
> *   In dust and ashes lie,*
> *What of the Smoker? Whither passed?*
> *   Ah, will he smoke no more?*

Not a man to be left empty-handed, le Gallienne continued:

> *. . . and when at length*
> *You lay me 'neath the yew,*
> *Forget not, O my friends, I pray,*
> *Pipes and tobacco too!*

A Grave Joke

When King James I died in 1625, tobacco's first archenemy was buried along with other monarchs in the royal church. But when Arthur Stanley, the dean of Westminster Abbey in London, went looking for the tomb two and a half centuries later the sarcophagus was not where he'd expected to find it. When he ultimately located what he believed to be the one, Stanley ordered it opened for verification. James was indeed within, but tucked next to him was a well-smoked clay pipe. Historians surmise that it had been put there by a pipe-smoking mortician with a delightfully ironic sense of humor.

© Kevin Gordon

THE LAST PIPE

When head is sick and brain doth swim,
And heavy hangs each unstrung limb,
'Tis sweet through smoke-puffs, wreathing slow,
To watch the firelight flash or glow.
As each soft cloud floats up on high,
Some worry takes its wings to fly;
And Fancy dances with the flame,
Who lay so labor-crammed and lame;
While the spent Will, the slack Desire,
Re-kindle at the dying fire,
And burn to meet the morrow's sun
With all its day's work to be done.

The tedious tangle of the Law,
Your work ne'er done without some flaw;
Those ghastly streets that drive one mad,
With children joyless, elders sad,
Young men unmanly, girls going by
Bold-voiced, with eyes unmaidenly;
Christ dead two thousand years agone,
And kingdom come still all unwon;
Your own slack self that will not rise
Whole-hearted for the great emprise,—
Well, all these dark thoughts of the day
As thin smoke's shadow drift away.

And all those magic mists unclose,
And a girl's face amid them grows,—
The very look she's wont to wear,
The wild rose blossoms in her hair,
The wondrous depths of her pure eyes,
The maiden soul that 'neath them lies,
That fears to meet, yet will not fly,
Your stranger spirit drawing nigh.
What if our times seem sliding down?
She lives, creation's flower and crown.
What if your way seems dull and long?
Each tiny triumph over wrong,
Each effort up through sloth and fear,
And she and you are brought more near.
So rapping out these ashes light,—
"My pipe, you've served me well to-night."

—*London Spectator*

Glossary

The vocabulary . . . is nervous and terse, but limited.
The selection of words would hardly lend itself to the
sending of general messages.

—SHERLOCK HOLMES
"The Valley of Fear"

Acorn: Another name for a pear-shaped bowl.

Aging: Last stage in preparation of tobacco prior to shipment to wholesalers. Cured leaves are stored in casks (hogsheads) and allowed to mellow.

Air-cured: Tobacco that has been dried naturally by hanging it in open-ventilated sheds.

Alderman: Ultralong pipe, usually clay.

Aromatic: A tobacco to which flavoring has been added.

Arrow: A tall, pear-bowled, half-bent pipe with round shank.

Auction: Wholesale selling of tobacco.

Bent: A curved pipe.

Billiard: A bowl shape.

Bit: The part of the pipe stem that goes in the mouth. It is also called a mouthpiece. The airhole may be flattened with a wide opening (wedge), round (orific), or on top (steck).

Bowl: Where the tobacco is burned. There are numerous shapes and sizes. (See chapter 5.)

Brandy glass: Pipe bowl shaped like a brandy glass, usually with round shank and bent or straight stem.

Briar: Hardwood pipe made from the white heather tree burl.

Bulldog: Hefty bowl with one or two grooves at the outermost bulge, usually with diamond shank, bent or straight, often with tapered stem. Also known as a squat.

Bullmoose: A very stout bulldog with a round, bent shank and a tapered bit.

Burl: A knobby growth from which all of a plant's roots extend.

Burley: A tobacco grown primarily in the Upper Midwest that is air-cured and used in blending.

Calabash: A pipe made from a South African gourd and fitted with a meerschaum bowl. Can also be made of briar.

Canadian: Long briar pipe with oval shank and short stem.

Cavendish: Sweetened Virginia tobacco that is ideal for blending.

Char: Burned tobacco that forms a crust (caking) on the inside walls of the pipe bowl.

Cherrywood: Tall pipe made of cherrywood; it looks like a small log with bark still attached.

Chimney: A pipe with a very tall bowl. Also called a stack.

Chubby: Squat, stout pipe, usually a pot or apple bowl, with a straight, large-diameter shank.

Churchwarden: A long pipe, usually of clay.

Clay: A clay pipe.

Crosby: Long pipe with billiard bowl; long, thin, round shank; and tapered stem. Preferred by and identified with Bing Crosby.

Curing: A process for drying tobacco leaves.

Cutty: A short pipe, usually clay. *Cutty* is Scottish for short.

Dottle: Unburned, often soggy tobacco in the bottom of the bowl.

Dudeen: Irish version of the cutty. Sometimes called "elfin" or "fairy pipe."

Ébauchon: The rough and unshaped wood that is turned into the bowl and shank of a briar pipe.

Écume de mer: French for meerschaum, meaning "sea foam."

Egg: Egg-shaped bowl.

Ferrule: Metal band around the shank of a pipe.

Flake: Finely and irregularly cut tobacco.

Flame grain: The pattern of the grain of a briar pipe that resembles a flame.

Flue-curing: Drying tobacco with artifical heat.

Four-square: Four-sided bowl, square shank, straight stem.

Freehand: Hand-carved, usually following the grain.

Heel: Inside bottom of a pipe bowl.

Hogshead: Approximately one thousand pounds of cured tobacco leaves.

Hookah: A large water pipe.

Horn: Resembles a bull's horn.

Latakia: Syrian tobacco used in blending.

Leaf: Tobacco before it is processed.

Liverpool: Like a Canadian, but with round shank and tapered stem.

Manzanita: A California briar.

Meerschaum: A white seaside mineral found primarily in Turkey that is light, porous, and easily carved into pipes; also used to line briar and calabash bowls.

Missouri Meerschaum: A corncob pipe. Also a trade name.

Mouthpiece: The pipe bit.

Narghile: A water pipe.

Nicotiana: Science's term for several kinds of tobacco. The one that is used for smoking is *N. tabacum.*

Nicotine: Tobacco's pleasure-producing main chemical ingredient.

Nose-warmer: A short pipe, usually bent.

Oom-Paul: Tall billiard, egg, or pot bowl with full bent, named after the first president of South Africa whose nickname was Uncle Paul ("Oom Paul" in the native language).

Oval: A bowl that is half elliptical, with the wider part of the bowl toward the shank. Also called a pocket pipe.

Panel: Flat-sided bowl.

Pear: Pear-shaped bowl.

Perique: Strong and flavorful Louisiana-grown tobacco used in the blending of aromatics.

Pipe mark: The hallmark of the pipe maker, usually initials.

Plug: Tobacco that is pressed into cakes or blocks.

Poker: Cylindrical bowl; looks like a judge's gavel.

Pot: Round bowl, bent or straight, round or oval shank.

Prince: Squat apple with flattened bottom; short, round shank; and long, tapered, slightly bent stem. Also called Prince of Wales, Prince Regent, and diplomat.

Quaint: Panel pipe with more than four sides.

Raw: Unprocessed tobacco.

Rhodesian: Squat, bulldog bowl with a bent diamond shank and a tapered stem.

Sax: Saxophone-shaped. An Oom-Paul.

Shag: Finely shredded pipe tobacco.

Shank: The part of the pipe between the bowl and the stem.

Stack: Very tall bowl, also called a chimney.

Stem: The part between the shank and the mouthpiece.

Tenon: The end of the stem that fits into the shank's mortise.

Topping: Trimming of the tobacco plant to maximize growth and to produce more desirable leaves.

Tube: Early form of pipe; also an archaic synonym for a pipe.

Turkish: Air-cured tobacco, also known as Oriental.

Woodstock: A Dublin bowl that tilts away from the smoker. The shank is usually oval. Also called a yachtsman.

Yard of clay: A clay pipe measuring thirty-six inches.

Zulu: Like a Woodstock but with the bowl tipped at a greater angle.

Further Reading

There upon a shelf was a formidable row of scrap-
books and books of reference . . . the pipe rack—even
the Persian slipper which contained the tobacco. . . .

—DR. JOHN H. WATSON
"The Empty House"

Books

Akehurst, B. C. *Tobacco.* New York: Humanities Press, 1968.

Apperson, G. L. *The Social History of Smoking.* New York: G. P. Putnam's Sons, 1916.

Ayto, Eric G. *Clay Tobacco Pipes.* Aylesbury, Buck., U.K.: Shire Publications, Ltd., 1979.

Beaumier, John Paul, and Lewis Camp. *The Pipe Smoker.* San Francisco: Harper & Row, 1980.

Brooks, Jerome E. *The Mighty Leaf.* Boston: Little, Brown and Company, 1952.

Dunhill, Alfred. *The Pipe Book.* London: Arthur Barker, Ltd., 1969.

Dunhill, Alfred H. *The Gentle Art of Smoking.* New York: G. P. Putnam and Sons, 1954.

Ehwa, Carl Jr. *The Book of Pipes and Tobacco.* New York: Random House, 1974.

Hacker, Richard Carleton. *The Ultimate Pipe Book.* Beverly Hills: Autumn Gold Publishing, 1984.

Heinmann, Robert. *Tobacco and Americans.* New York: McGraw-Hill, 1960.

Herment, Georges. *The Pipe.* New York: Simon & Schuster, 1957.

Knight, Joseph, ed. *Pipe and Pouch.* Boston: Joseph Knight Company, 1895.

Robert, Joseph. *The Tobacco Kingdom.* Durham, N.C.: Duke University Press, 1938.

Sherman, Milton M. *All About Tobacco.* Woodside, N.Y.: P. M. Sherman Corp., 1970.

Weber, Carl. *The Pleasures of Pipe Smoking.* New York: Bantam Books, Inc., 1965.

Monograph

Holmes, Sherlock. "Upon the Distinction between the Ashes of the Various Tobaccos." London: Manuscript, date not known. This reference source has been the object of intense searching by tobacconists, law enforcement agencies, and Holmesian scholars for more than a century.

Sources

A trusty comrade is always of use.

—SHERLOCK HOLMES
"The Man with the Twisted Lip"

*A*s this book has demonstrated, pipe smoking is a pleasure that may be pursued alone or in the company of a friend or two. However, writing a book on the subject is a challenge that is best undertaken with all the help you can find. In that I have been fortunate, so I herewith gratefully acknowledge the work of Kevin Gordon as both illustrator and photographer.

Gail Eveland Hebert went where few women have dared to go by traveling in cyberspace in search of whatever might be out there on the topic. Additional valuable Website material was provided by another Internet veteran, Al Leibholz.

Help was also happily rendered by my literary agent, Jake Elwell, who let me borrow rare volumes from his collection of pipe books. Thanks, too, to Sam Hall for printed materials.

Neither is it possible to cover the field of pipes and the subjects of pipe smoking, pipe enthusiasts, pipe history, pipe trivia, and everything else about pipes without recourse to the frequently mentioned *Pipe Smoker's Ephemeris* and its tireless editor-publisher, Tom Dunn; so many thanks to him.

I am also indebted to the following individuals and firms for providing information and illustrative material: David Edel, International Association of Pipe Smokers Clubs; Bill Feuerbach III, S. M. Frank & Company; Jennifer L. Hisserich, Missouri Meerschaum, Inc.; and the

Kirsten Pipe Company, Inc., Seattle, WA; *Ser Jacapo della Gemma,* Italy, and Marble Arch Ltd., Rockville Centre, NY *(Ser Jacapo pipes);* Ashton Distributors, Philadelphia, PA; Alfred Dunhill Pipes Ltd., London, U.K.; James Norman, Ltd., New York, NY *(Barling and Caminetto pipes);* Peterson of Dublin, Ireland; Pipestone Indian Shrine Association and the U.S. National Parks Service *(calumet pipes);* Jean-Paul Barrod, *Société des pipes* Butz-Choquin, France; Missouri Meerschaum Company, Washington, Missouri; Savinelli Inc., USA, Morrisville, NC; and Kaywoodie/Yellow Bole/Medico, Peekskill, NY.

It is impossible to express in words my gratitude to Joseph Peretti and the staff of L. J. Peretti Company for their assistance during a day of photography and other forms of poking around in the pipes of their famous store in Park Square, Boston.

For your assistance in exploring the world of pipes, here is a representative sampling of sources:

Clubs and Organizations

Arrowhead Pipe Club
Tom Medford, President
647 South Saginaw Street
Flint, MI 48502

Barcelona Pipa Club
Placa Reial, 3 pral
08002 Barcelona
Spain

Bay Area Pipe Club
Marty Pulvers
4 Embarcadero Center
San Francisco, CA 94111

Bombay Cigar Society
209 Avenue "I"
Redondo Beach, CA 90277

Briar Society of Washington
    College
350 Washington Avenue
Chestertown, MD 21620-1197

The Briar Squires
P.O. Box 136
Milwaukee, WI 53201-0136

Calabash Cavaliers Pipe Club
P.O. Box 219
Galveston, IN 46832

Carolina Briar Friars
228 South Clarkson Street
Charlotte, NC 28202

Central Oklahoma Pipe Enthusiasts
(C.O.P.E.)
P.O. Box 7034
Moore, OK 73153-7034

Chesapeake Pipe Club
808 Mockingbird Lane, Apt. 202
Towson, MD 21286

Chicagoland Pipe Collectors Club
2947 Edison Street
Blue Island, IL 60406

Civil War Smokers
1925 Weltshire Drive
Davenport, IA 52806

Conclave of Richmond Pipe
    Smokers
P.O. Box 34023
Richmond, VA 23234

Indiana Briar Friars
Route 1, Box 78
Arlington, IN 46104

International Association of Pipe
    Smokers Clubs
3896 Bay Road
Saginaw, MI 48603

New York Pipe Club
P.O. Box 265
Gracie Station, New York, NY 10028

Nordic Smokers Guild
Ellekrattet 18
2950 Vedback
42 89 44 02, Denmark

North American Society of Pipe
    Collectors
P.O. Box 9642
Columbus, OH 43209-9642

Ohio Pipe Collectors
P.O. Box 9642
Columbus, OH 43209

Original Grumblers Club
1427 Lexington Avenue
St. Paul, MN 55113

Peninsula Pipe Club
at the British Bankers Club
El Camino Real and Santa Cruz
    Avenue
Menlo Park, CA

Peterson Smokers' Guild
Peterson House
Dublin, Ireland

The Pipe Club of London
9 Frances Street
Chesham, Buck. HP5 3EQ
England

Pipe Collectors Club of America
P.O. Box 5179
Woodbridge, VA 22194-5179

Pipe Collectors International
1715 Promenade Center
Richardson, TX 75080

Santa's Smokers
P.O. Box 55028
North Pole, AK 99705

Southeastern Michigan Pipe Club
7127 Elmhurst
West Bloomfield, MI 48322

South Florida Briar Brotherhood
P.O. Box 450967
Sunrise, FL 33345-0967

Southwest Pipe and Cigar League
11407 Culver Boulevard
Los Angeles, CA 90066

St. Louis Gateway Area Pipe Club
14070 New Halls Ferry
Florissant, MO 63033

Tampa Bay Pipe Club
119 Bullard Parkway
Temple Terrace, FL 33617

Tri-Cities Pipe Club
3986 Bay Road
Saginaw, MI 48603

Universal Coterie of Pipe Smokers
Tom Dunn, President
20–37 120th Street
College Point, NY 11356

The Up Down Sons of Briars
1550 North Wells Street
Chicago, IL 60610

Wisconsin Briar Friars
1613 North Peach
Marshfield, WI 54449

Corncob Pipes

Missouri Meerschaum Company
P.O. Box 226
Washington, MO 63090

Internet Sources

Internet Pipes Mailgroup
Steve Masticola, Moderator
masticol@scr.siemens.com

Organization of Online Pipe
   Smokers
http://www.fujipub.com.ooops

Pipes Web Page
http://www.pipes.org

Museums

Duke Homestead State Historic
   Site & Tobacco Museum
2828 Duke Homestead Road
Durham, North Carolina

North Carolina Collection Library
   and Gallery
University of North Carolina
Chapel Hill, North Carolina
(There's a statue of Raleigh smok-
ing a long clay.)

Paul's Pipe Shop and Museum
647 South Saginaw Street
Flint, Michigan

Tobacco Farm Life Museum
Highway 301 North
Kenly, North Carolina

Publications

Agricultural and Mechanical Gazette
47758 Hickory, Apt. 22305
Wixom, MI 48393

Pipe Friendly Magazine
P.O. Box 13781
Torrance, CA 90503

The Pipe Smoker's Ephemeris
20-37 120th Street
College Point, NY 11356

Pipes and Tobaccos
3000 Highwoods Boulevard
Suite 300
Raleigh, NC 27604-1029

Smoke
130 West 42nd Street, Suite 1050
New York, NY 10036
or, Box 56510
Boulder, CO 80323-6510

Smoke Rings
2419 Smallman Street
Pittsburgh, PA 15222

Smoker's Advocate
Phillip Morris USA
120 Park Avenue
New York, NY 10017

Smokeshop
Lockwood Trade Journal Co., Inc.
130 West 42nd Street, Suite 1050
New York, NY 10036-7899

*Southwest Pipe and Cigar League
    Gazette*
11407 Culver Boulevard
Los Angeles, CA 90066

Tobacconist
3000 Highlands Boulevard, Suite
    300
Raleigh, NC 27604

Tobacco Times
3161 Maple Drive Northeast
Atlanta, GA 30305

Pipemaking Supplies

American Smoking Pipe Company
HC-88, Box 223
30 Tall Oaks
Pocono Lake, PA 18347

PIMO, Inc.
Butternut Lane, P.O. Box 2043
Manchester Center, VT 05255

Repair and Refurbishing Services

CALIFORNIA

Sherlock's Haven
275 Battery Street
San Francisco, CA 94111

Jim Benjamin
12199 Avenida Consentido
San Diego, CA 92128

COLORADO

Matt's Pipe Rejuvenation
    Company
1303 Columbine Street, Suite 103
Denver, CO 80206

NEW YORK

Pipes Unlimited
19 Auburn Avenue
Utica, NY 13501

OHIO

Unger's Pipe Refurbishing
800 Franklin Avenue
Columbus, OH 43205

Tim West, Inc.
1588 Grayling Court
Columbus, OH 43253

OKLAHOMA

Bill's Pipe Repair
2509 Southwest 52nd Place
Oklahoma City, OK 73119

PENNSYLVANIA

American Smoking Pipe Company
HC-88, Box 223
30 Tall Oaks
Pocono Lake, PA 18347

VERMONT

J.T.&D. Cooke
R.F.D. 1, Box 1022
East Fairfield, VT 05448-9801
(802) 849-6272

Tobacco Industry Information

Retail Tobacco Dealers Association
107 East Baltimore Street
Baltimore, MD 21202

Index

Abbott and Costello Meet the Invisible Man, 164
Accompaniments, 139–140
"Acrostic", 116
Actors, 59
    See also specific individuals
Adam Norbrook, 56
Addison, Charles, 137
Adham, 38
Advertising, 54, 109–111, 147, 149
Aldermen, 34
Alfred, Lord Tennyson, 57, 59, 138, 158
Alfred Club, 138
All Fools, 165
Andrassy, Count, 75, 76
Andy Hardy, 150
Antismoking movement, 5, 7, 55, 94,
    120, 121, 140–141, 147
    See also King James I
Apperson, G.L., 37, 54, 55, 170
Apple, 66
Armellini, 99
Aromatics, 122
Ascorti, 99
Ashton, 99
Astaire, Fred, 59
Ayto, Eric G., 33

Bacon, Francis, 15, 21, 151
Baine, John, 93
Baker Street Journal, 164
Baldo Baldi, 99
"Ballad of the Pipe, The", 7
Barling, 99, 181
Barrie, James, 59
Barrymore, John, 59
BBB Pipes, 99, 108
Beaumier, John Paul, 26, 52, 146, 168
Beaumont, Hugh, 149
Benchley, Robert, 4, 128, 151
Ben-Sim Company, 114
Ben Wade, 102

Bergman, Ingrid, 95, 150
Billiard, 66
Bit, 66
*Black Elk Speaks: Being the Life Story of a
    Holy Man of Oglala Sioux* (Nei-
    hardt), 26
Blends, 122, 124–126
Bogart, Humphrey, 95, 150
"Bogeying", 150
Bonheur, Rosa, 172
Book Hunter's Holiday, A (Rosenbach),
    178
Boone, Daniel, 43
Bouffard, 28
Bouffardi, Jean Nepoma, 28
Bowie, Jim, 43, 151
Bowl, 32, 63, 64–65
    filling the, 94
    Kirsten, 113
Brands
    collectible, 181–182
    mass-market, 123
Breaking in, 93
Brebbia, 100
Brett, Jeremy, 59, 149, 164
Briar calabash pipe, 81
Briar pipe, 88
    breaking in, 93
    description of, 63–69
    makers, 99–102
    making a, 68–74
    origins of, 35–37
    sweetening, 98–99
Bright tobacco, 118–119
British Empire, 38–40
Brooks, Jerome E., 21, 119, 127–128
Brown, Henry E., 61, 83
Brown, Thomas, 168
Bruyère, 37
Brylon, 112
Buckley, Elton J., 87
Bulldog, 66

Bulwer-Lytton, Lord, 7
Burl, 69, 72
Burley tobacco, 119, 120, 121, 122
Burl grain, 73
"Burnout", 96
Burton, Richard, 166
Butz-Choquin, 99
Byron, Lord, 57, 138, 151

Cake, 123, 131
Caking, proper, 93, 98
Calabash pipe, 3, 5, 62, 79–80, 164
    making a, 80
Calumet pipe, 25–28, 55
Caminetto, 100
Camp, Lewis, 26, 52, 146, 168
Campus life, 136–137
Canadian, 65, 66
Cannon, 59
CAO Meerschaum, 114
Carburetor, 108
Care, long-term, 98
Cartier, Jacques, 25
Carved finish, 74
Casablanca, 95, 150
Casing, 122
Castello, 100
Catlin, George, 28
Catlinite, 28
Cavendish tobacco, 119, 122
Cesare, 100
Chamber, 65
Chancellor, John, 149
Chapman, George, 165
Chapuis-Comoy, 100
Charatan, 100, 181
Cherrywood pipe, 62, 74–75
Chibouk, 40
Chop cut, 122
Christie, Agatha, 29
Churchwarden, 34, 65, 164
Cigarettes, 54, 55, 128, 150, 167
    health effects of, 142, 143–144

popularity of, 46–47, 88, 136, 171
    smoker personality, 52
Cigars, 54, 55, 65, 97, 107, 128, 132,
    139, 150, 166, 167
    humidor for, 129
    popularity of, 44, 46, 48, 88, 175
Civil War, 43, 44, 88
Clay pipe, 36, 40, 43, 62, 89
    care, 99
    leading names in, 113
    making a, 81–82
    origin of, 31–35
Clay Tobacco Pipes (Ayto), 33
Clemens, Samuel Langhorne. *See*
    Twain, Mark
Clerc, E., 76–77
Clubs and shows, 187
Coffeehouses, 137
Cohan, George M., 46
Collecting
    pipes, 178–182
    tobacco tins, 182–186
"Collector, The", 179
Colman, Ronald, 170
Comoy's, 100, 108
Companion, pipe smoker's, 131
Compleat Angler *(Walton), 31*
*Complete Guide to Collecting Antique
    Pipes, A* (Rapaport), 182
Connery, Sean, 29
Conrad, William, 59, 149
Cooper, Thomas, 56
Corncob pipe, 82–83, 115
    care, 98
    making a, 84–85
    origins of, 43–44
Costello, Lou, 164
Crisp, Donald, 5
Criswell, Eleanor, 52–53
Criswell survey, 52–53, 144, 168
Criteria, collecting, 180–181
Crockett, Davy, 43, 152
Cronkite, Walter, 4, 149

Crosby, Bing, 5, 59, 152
Cross-cut grain, 73
Cube cut, 122
Curing, 72–73, 120–121
Cutty pipe, 34, 65

Dale, Thomas, 13, 17
Danish pipe, 34
Davis, Richard Harding, 4
Defore, Don, 149
De La Concha, 124, 126
de Leon, Ponce, 25
Dickens, Charles, 34, 170
Diversity, 139–140
Dottle, 91, 97, 131, 141
Doyle, Arthur Conan, 50, 80, 149, 164
    See also Holmes, Sherlock
"Dreamer's Pipe, The", 79
Drinkless pipe, 107–108
Dublin, 67
Dudeen, 65
Duffield, Samuel W., 57
Dunhill, 2, 90, 100–101
    dating, 181–182
    tins, 186
    tobacco, 126
Dunhill, Alfred, 100, 178
Dunn, Tom, 174, 185
Dupin, Amandine Aurore Lucie, 171
Durante, Jimmy "The Schnozz", 79–80

Ébauchon, 72–73
Écume de mer, 40
Einstein, Albert, 51, 153
Elfin pipe, 34
Elliott, Denholm, 50
Emerson, Ralph Waldo, 59, 153
Emptying, pipe, 97
England, 10–13, 14–17, 21
English tobacco, 122
Ennis, Robert S., 164
Equipment
    freshness, 128–130

pipe, 130–132
Esserman, Richard, 182, 186

Fairy pipe, 34
Fell, Sarah, 169
Fenwick, Millicent, 171
Fermi, Enrico, 51
Filters, 69, 107, 111
Finishing, 73–74
Finney, Albert, 29
"Fitz-Boodle Papers", 165–166
Fitzgerald, Barry, 5, 56, 153
Fitzgerald, F. Scott, 59
Flake cut, 122
Flame grain, 73
Flush, 65
Flynn, Errol, 5, 59
Foot, 65
Ford, Harrison, 50
Ford, John, 56
Fothergill, Samuel, 170
Fourneau, 28
Fox, George, 169
Franklin, Benjamin, 41
Freehand, 67
Freshness, maintaining, 128–130
Frost, Robert, 85

Gable, Clark, 5, 59, 154
Gadgets, 130–132
Gambier, 40
Garbett, Jane, 170
Gargan, William, 147
Garth, Samuel, 22, 31
GBD, 101
Gift, purchase as, 115–116
Gillette, William, 59, 164
Gormley, John J., 1, 55
Grahame, Kenneth, 138
Grain, 73
Great Depression, 47, 107
Grenville, Richard, 11, 13
Grossich, Mark, 175

Groves, Leslie, 51
Guidelines, smoking, 140–141
Guilerman, Arthur, 179
Gunsmoke, 59
Gwenn, Edmund, 150

Hacker, Richard Carleton, 48, 60, 92, 95, 133, 182
Hainer, Cathy, 177
Haliburton, Thomas Chandler, 53
Hall, John, 163, 164
Hariot, Thomas, 11–12, 13
Harrison, William, 11
Hawkins, John, 10–11
Head, 64
Health effects, 141–144
Hemingway, Ernest, 59, 171
Henry, Patrick, 41
Hentzler, Paul, 31–32
Herment, Georges, 60, 69, 82, 133, 146
Hobbes, Thomas, 31
Hogsheads, 42
Holiday Inn, 59
Holmes, Sherlock, 3, 50, 80, 81, 129, 130, 149
    as most famous pipe smoker, 161–165
    Rathbone as, 5, 59, 91, 106–107, 183
    types of pipes, 62–63, 139
Hookah, 38, 40
Hound of the Baskervilles, The (Doyle), 161
Howard, Ronald, 149
How Green Was My Valley, 5, 156
Huckleberry Finn (Twain), 146
Humidor, 128–129

Image
    social, 52–53
    traditional, 50–52, 147
Immortality, pipe, 53–55
Imported tobaccos, 124

International pipes, 38–40
Internet, 176–177
"Irish Hubub", 14
Iwan Ries & Company, 126

Jamestown colony, 13
James Upshall, 102
Jeffers, H. Paul
    Holmes collection, 3, 182–183
    love of pipes, 4–8
    personal pipes of, 2–4
Jobey, 101
John Pollock & Company, 113
Johnson, Samuel, 29
Jones, Thomas, 117
Joyce, James, 106, 155

Kapp & Peterson, 106
Kaywoodie, 89, 101, 112, 182
    success of, 107–111
King Edward VII, 166–167
King James I, 16, 21, 29, 47, 55, 147
    death of, 193
Kipling, Rudyard, 59, 166
Kirsten, 112–113
Kirsten, F.K., 112–113
Knight of the Burning Pestle, The, 165
Kocoum, 13
Koet, Captain, 11
Kowates, Karl, 75, 76

Lamb, Charles, 59, 155
Lane, Ralph, 11, 12, 13
"Last Pipe, The", 194
Latakia tobacco, 119, 120
Leave It to Beaver, 149
le Gallienne, Richard, 7, 192
Lepeltier, 113
Lewis, Sinclair, 59
Light Guitar, The (Guilerman), 179
Lighting, 94–95
Lip, 66, 108
L.J. Peretti, 2, 115, 124

London Meerschaum, Ltd., 114
Long cut, 122
Lorenzo Pipes, 101
Lorillard, Pierre, 42, 43
Lowell, James Russell, 57, 78
M&L Trading Company, 114
MacArthur, Douglas, 44, 156
MacMurray, Fred, 5, 50, 149
Maker's marks, 31, 89–90
Maltese Falcon, The, 150
Manhattan Briar Pipe Company, 111
Manufacturers, 99–102, 113, 114
Marketing, 54, 109–111, 147, 149
Marshal, Thomas, 107
Martin, Billy, 147
Martin Kane, Private Eye, 147, 149
Maryland tobacco, 119
Masculine bonding, 137–138
Matlick, Dayton, 144, 175
Matowaka, 13
Maugham, Somerset, 59, 155
Maury, James, 41
McLaglen, Victor, 56
McNeil, Mary, 118, 123
Medico, 89, 107, 111–112
Meerschaum pipe, 3, 40, 57, 78–79
  care, 98
  description of, 75–77
  making a, 77–78
  reliable sources of, 114
Melville, Herman, 59, 155
Men's clubs, 137–138
Middleton, William, 11
Mighty Leaf, The (Brooks), 21, 119,
  127–128
Miracle on Thirty-Fourth Street, 150
Missouri Meerschaum, 44, 85, 115, 156
Missouri Meerschaum Company, 43, 83
Moisture, problem of, 103–107,
  112–113
Molly, Pheasy, 170
Moore, Clement, 59–60, 149–150
Mortise-and-tenon joint, 65

"Motto for a Tobacco Jar", 126
Mouthpiece, 63, 66
Movies, 149–150
Mr. Punch's Pocket-Book, 167
Munby, A.J., 36–37
Murder on the Orient Express (Christie), 29
"My Friendly Pipe", 47
"My Old Clay Pipe", 35
My Three Sons, 149

Names
  manufacturers', 99–102, 113, 114
  pipe, 28–31, 38, 40
Narghile, 40
Native Americans, 10–11, 25–28, 32, 55
Neihardt, John G., 26
Nero Wolfe, 59
New Jersey Briar Pipe Company, 112
News articles, 177–178
Newton, Isaac, 31
Nicot, Jean, 22
Nicotiana, 18
Nicotiana rustica, 118
Nicotiana tabacum, 118, 119
Nicotine, 22
Night and Morning (Bulwer-Lytton), 7
Nitwits, The, 164
Nolan, Lloyd, 147
Nording, 101

O'Casey, Sean, 106
"Ode to My Pipe", 23
O'Hara, John, 4, 59
Old Crock, 138
"Old Pipe of Mine", 1
"Old Sweetheart of Mine, An", 168
"140 Different Varieties", 163, 164
"On the Gift of a Meerschaum Pipe", 78
Oppenheimer, Robert, 51
Organization of Online Pipe Smokers
  (OoOPS), 176–177
Organizations, 176–177
Orific lip, 66

Ozzie and Harriet, 149

Pacific Briar Company, 108
Packaging, 123–126
Packing, proper, 93
Painters, 59
Palissandre, 75
Paper on Tobacco, A, 53
Parker-Hardcastle, 101
Parson's Cause, 41
Payton, Katherine, 170
Peace pipe, 25–26
Peisly, Mary, 170
Penn, William, 31
Perique tobacco, 119, 121
Pershing, John J. "Black Jack", 44, 156
Personalities, famous, 150–160
    See also specific individuals
Personality types, 51–52, 143–144
Peterson, 2, 5, 101, 163, 181
    moisture problem, 103–107
    special pipes, 89
Peterson, Charles, 104
Pfeiffe, 29, 31
Phifa, 29
Pib, 29, 31
Pibe, 29, 31
Picasso, Pablo, 171
Pidgeon, Walter, 5, 156
Pipe, love of, 4–8
Pipe, The (Herment), 60, 146
Pipe Book, The (Dunhill), 178
Pipe cleaner, 97, 98, 132
Pipe Dan, 102
Pipe racks, 98, 132–133
Pipes and Tobaccos, 144, 175
Pipes Digest, 176
Pipe Smoker, The (Beaumier and Camp), 26, 52, 146, 168
Pipe Smoker's Ephemeris, The, 173, 174, 182, 185, 186
Pipe smoking

calming effects of, 55–56, 95–96, 146–147
history of, 10–17
increase in, 47, 175–176
location for, 140–141
origins of, 24–25
time for, 138–139
Pipestone, 28
Pipes Unlimited, 114
Pipe tobacco, making, 121–123
    See also Tobacco
"Pipe Wears Many Hats, The", 51
"Pipe You Make Yourself, The", 83
Plague pipe, 34
Pleasures of Pipe Smoking, The (Weber), 53, 62, 91, 133, 140, 143, 146
Plug, 122–123
Pocahontas, 13–14, 17
Poirot, Hercule, 29
Poker, 67
Pompadour, Madame, 172
Pot, 67
Pouch, tobacco, 129–130
Powhatan, 13
Preben Holm, 102
Presidential pipers, 160–161
Price, Thomas, 11
Priestley, J.B., 126
Prince, 2, 67
Proprietary pipes, 115
Publications, 175–176

Queen Elizabeth I, 10, 12–13, 14, 16, 51
Queen Victoria, 34–35, 40, 166
Quiet Man, The, 5, 56, 153
Quotations, 187–191

"Radiator" stem, 113
Radice, 102
Raleigh, Sir Walter, 51, 81, 102, 103
    beheaded, 16, 31, 147
    introduces tobacco, 10, 12–13, 17, 29, 38, 42

"lights a candle", 14, 22, 174, 191
smoking habits, 14–16, 47
Rapaport, Benjamin, 182
Rathbone, Basil, 5, 59, 89, 91, 106–107, 163, 183
Rave, Hermann, 7
Reamer, 131
Reiss-Premier Pipe Company, 108
Restoration, 181
Ribbon cut, 122
Rich, Barnaby, 14
Riley, James Whitcomb, 168
Ring gauge, 65
Robinson, Edward G., 59, 157
Rockwell, Norman, 59, 157
Roles, 16, 42
Rolfe, John, 13–14, 17, 20, 43, 103
Roll-up pouch, 130
Romeo and Juliet, 102–103
Roosevelt, Theodore "Teddy", 3, 4, 59
Ropp, 102
Rosenbach, A.S.W., 178
Rosewood pipe, 75
Round pouch, 130
Royal Meerschaum Pipe Company, 114

Saddle, 66
"Sam Slick", 53
Sand, George, 171
Sandblasted finish, 74
Sandburg, Carl, 59, 158
Sasieni, 90, 102, 181
Savinelli, 102
"Sea foam", 40, 114
Seconds, 90
"Selecting Pipe Tobacco", 118
Selection, pipe, 91–93
as gift, 115–116
Shag cut, 91, 122, 163, 164
Shakespeare, William, 15, 16, 102, 146
Shank, 65
Shapes and styles, 66–67
Shaping, 73

Shean, Burton, 51–52, 143
Sherlock Holmes Classic Collection, 89
Shields, Arthur, 56
Signature pipe, 31
S.M. Frank and Company, 111–112
Smith, John, 13, 14, 17
Smoke, 175–176
"Smoker's Calendar, The", 134
Smoking, proper, 95–97
preparation for, 92–95
Smoking and Health, 142, 143
Smoking cool, 96
Smollett, Tobias, 36
Smooth finish, 74
Social History of Smoking, The (Apperson), *37, 54, 170*
Society of Tobacco-pipe-makers, 29
Spanish tobacco, 19, 20
Stalin, Joseph, 55
Stanley, Arthur, 193
Steck lip, 66
Stein, Gertrude, 139, 171
Steinbeck, John, 2, 4, 59
Stem, 32, 63, 65–66
Stereotypes, 50–52
Stogie. *See* Cigars
Stone, Lewis, 150
Straight grain, 73
Surgeon general's report, 142
Surveys, 51–53
Sweetening, 98–99
Symbolism, 27, 146
Synge, John Milton, 106
Tale of Two Cities, A (Dickens), 170
Tamper, 131
Tarlton, Richard, 14
Taylor, Mrs. Zachary, 171
Television, 149
Teller, Edward, 51
Thackeray, William Makepeace, 47, 54, 165
Tibbe, Henry, 43, 83, 84, 85
Tobacco

auction, 121
cultivation and harvesting, 120
curing, 120–121
cutting, 122–123
history of, 10–18, 20–22
imported, 124
kinds of, 118–119
as legal tender, 17–18, 41
making pipe, 121–123
mixing and blending, 122
origins of, 18–20
packaging, 123–126
trade in, 17–18, 42–43
Tobacconist, 175
Tobacconists, 31, 94, 115, 129
Tobacco tins, collecting, 182–186
Tolkien, J.R.R., 59
"Topping", 120
Touba, 38
Tracy, Lee, 147
Tracy, Spencer, 50, 158
Turkish tobacco, 119
Turner, Hy, 4
Twain, Mark, 4, 59, 122, 145–146
corncob pipe and, 44, 85
Peterson and, 89, 106, 107
Ultimate Pipe Book, The (Hacker), 48, 60, 92, 95–96, 182
United States
between the wars, 44–48
corn cob pipe and, 43–44
pipe history, 40–43
Ural Pipes, 114
Used pipe, 91

Van Fleet, A.B., 35
van Gogh, Vincent, 59, 159
Velez, Lupe, 172, 174
Vigée-Lebrun, Élisabeth, 172
Virginia colony, 13–14, 17–18, 20–22
Virginia tobacco, 18, 20–21, 118–119, 120, 121, 122

"Visit from St. Nicholas, A", 59–60, 149–150
Vonnegut, Kurt, 59

Wally Frank, Ltd., 101
Walton, Izaak, 31
Washington, George, 41–42
Water pipe, 38, 40
Watson, Dr., 164–165
See also Holmes, Sherlock
Wayne, John, 56
Weber, Carl, 69, 92, 101, 144
Pleasures of Pipe Smoking, The, 53, 62, 91, 133, 140, 143, 146
Wedge lip, 66
Wetness, problem of, 103–107, 112–113
Wheeler and Woolsey, 164
Whitmore, James, 59
William DeMuth and Company, 111
Wilson, Dooley, 95
"Wits' Recreation", 17
W.O. Larsen, 101
Women, 47, 53
pipes and, 165–168
pipe-smoking, 168–172
Wonderful World of Pipes, 51
Wood, for making pipes, 75
Wooden pipe. *See* Briar pipe
Woolsey, Robert, 164
World War I, 44, 46–47, 88, 137
World War II, 47, 108–109
Writers, 57, 59
Wynter, Andrew, 23

Yard of clay, 34
Yeats, William Butler, 106
Yello-Bole, 89
success of, 107–111

Zenith, 113
Zippered top pouch, 130